"*Innately* message i thesis that you are love, and documenting it from many sources, author ever read. Its ll. Stating her

Jan Denise locates the anti-thesis, that we are not 'good enough,' in our evolutionary, religious, and psychological history. Vulnerably using her personal history as the narrative thread, and weaving in the experiences of her clients, Denise eloquently describes the appalling negative impact of trying to be 'good enough' on our personal and relational lives and its debilitating impact on society. But she does not leave us with a scholarly analysis only. She closes the book with concrete processes of discovering our innate goodness and experiencing ourselves as 'love.'"

—**Harville Hendrix, Ph.D.**, coauthor of
Receiving Love: Transform Your Relationship
by Letting Yourself Be Loved with Helen LaKelly Hunt

"*Innately Good* is an absolutely wonderful book, full of wisdom, great stories, and the kind of truth that will set you free."

—**Christiane Northrup, M.D.**, author of
Mother-Daughter Wisdom, The Wisdom of Menopause, and
Women's Bodies, Women's Wisdom

"Jan Denise takes the work out of finding the path to who we truly are through this beautiful book: She dismantles "the lie" that we are not enough. She asks us to see 'the dream' of being pure love as a reality we can grasp. And, she shows us how to surrender to the pure love we are, always have been, and will continue to be."

—**David Essel,** author, television and radio host,
adjunct professor at Edison State College, Fort Myers, FL

"With a clear eye and a warm style, Jan Denise frankly sympathizes with our human need to be accepted and found 'worthy,' then cuts through the myths we want so desperately to believe: that 'stuff' will make us happy, that love can be accumulated from the outside. Whatever the reader's personal belief system, there is much in *Innately Good* that we ought to consider in our efforts to live more simply good, compassionate and happy lives."

—Ann L. Weber, Ph.D., author of
Perspectives on Close Relationships and *Psychology: Core Concepts.*

"In *Innately Good,* Jan Denise shines a clear and powerful spotlight on a critical epidemic of our time—the widespread disease of feeling, and believing, that one is not good enough. This is the debilitating root of so much mental, emotional, and spiritual suffering . . . and physical illness as well. With eloquence and grace—born from the crucible of her own self-healing—Jan skillfully and compassionately guides readers on the hero's journey from shame and isolation to the discovery of the true Self, filled with radiance, love, and possibility. This is an important and deeply inspiring book. A rare gift."

—Jeremy Geffen, M.D., FACP, author of
The Journey Through Cancer:
Healing and Transforming the Whole Person

Innately Good

DISPELLING

THE

MYTH

THAT

YOU'RE

NOT

Jan Denise

Health Communications, Inc.
Deerfield Beach, Florida

www.hcibooks.com

To protect the identity of certain people, some names and identifying characteristics have been changed.

Library of Congress Cataloging-in-Publication Data

Denise, Jan.
  Innately good : dispelling the myth that you're not / Jan Denise.
        p. cm.
    Includes bibliographical references and index.
    ISBN-13: 978-0-7573-0742-3 (trade paper)
    ISBN-10: 0-7573-0742-6 (trade paper)
      1. Good and evil.   2. Human beings.   3. Self-esteem.   I. Title.
  BJ1406.D46 2008
  158.1—dc22

                                                                    2008034243

Publisher: Health Communications, Inc.
            3201 S.W. 15th Street
            Deerfield Beach, FL 33442–8190

Cover design by Andrea Perrine Brower
Interior design and formatting by Lawna Patterson Oldfield

TO KNOWING LOVE,

THE GOODNESS WITHIN,

YOURS, AND MINE, AND OURS

CONTENTS

Part Three: The Truth—We Are Innately Good

Part Four: Being Who We Are . . .
It Means Overcoming Our Separateness

ACKNOWLEDGMENTS

I THANK THE *following friends:*

Thomas Hawkins for his friendship and for inspiring *Innately Good* with his genius, kindness, and questions.

Brenda Bender, Michael Daube, Mary Ann Hastings, Connie Lysko, Bill Marsiglio, and Pat Zwirz for their friendship and feedback on my work in progress.

H. C. Arbuckle III, Jessica Burtch, Ben Campen, Larry Dargie, Linda English, Bob Friedman, Glenn Grace, Glad Faith Klassen, Richard Malanchuk, Michael Murphy, Pat Nebel, Rosita Perez, Sandy Thompson, Charles Worthington, and Mark Zivojnovich for their ongoing friendship and support.

The team at HCI for publishing *Innately Good*: Pat Holdsworth for opening the door, Peter Vegso for letting me in, and Allison Janse for helping me to improve on what I offered them.

My mom who wanted more for me, and my dad who was content to love me as I was. They gave all they had to give. And I wish to honor their love by doing the same.

My husband, best friend, and spiritual partner Horace Osborne Ferguson III—aka Sam and Baby Precious—for sharing all of life and love with me.

INTRODUCTION

A SCIENTIST, GOD DID NOT LEAVE
OUR GOODNESS TO CHANCE. AN ARTIST, HE
CONTRASTED GOOD WITH EVIL, CERTAINTY
WITH MYSTERY. AND CHOICE IS THE LIFE
HE BREATHED INTO HIS CREATION.

—JAN DENISE

IN A SEA of self-help, swimming with bigger and smarter fish, I will be so bold as to isolate the one thing that spawned humankind's cries for salvation. Then I will label it a lie. I will explain where the lie came from and why we mostly still believe it. And I will do my best to convince you that, despite any and all evidence to the contrary, you are all that is good—not that you *can* be, or that you *will* be when you meet certain criteria, but that you are *innately* good, innately love, innately more than you ever dreamed of being.

Eons ago, our survival depended on being sensitive to rejection— without the protection of the clan, we were literally dead meat.

But what used to save our hides has become our worst enemy. We are biologically programmed to sense rejection as a sign that something is wrong with us; because we grow up with words like "no" and "bad" and "evil," unconscious feelings of inferiority are universal. Whether we realize it consciously or not, we are driven to prove to ourselves and to the world that we are worthwhile.

My own life reads like a textbook example. I grew up feeling inferior (though my insecurity was sometimes read as snobbiness). Then, after years of feeling sexually undesirable to my husband, at the age of twenty-four I got up the nerve to divorce him. That's when—with nobody to do it for me and nobody to blame for not doing it myself—I diligently set out to prove my worth. I went back to school, started earning more money than my ex-husband, bought my first new car, built a house, and sculpted my body at the gym (I was like a kid in a candy store and, without realizing it, I continued to base much of my self-image on a man finding me desirable). I read self-help books and sought professional guidance and approval. I took pride (a red flag I missed) in wanting to be the best I could be.

And as soon as I had my own affairs in order—which *really* meant after I had proven my worth—I wanted to help others: food for the hungry and jobs for anybody who wanted to work. *In effect, I postponed living my truth until I had demonstrated my worth . . . but I could not really demonstrate my worth without living my truth.* My aspirations were high, and my intentions, as far as I knew, were honorable, but I didn't have a foundation for them.

I wanted all the success the world had to offer *and* I wanted to be a "saint" . . . and, without looking like I was trying too hard, I wanted to be desired.

The magical milestone of "success" slipped in and out of my grasp. Just about the time I thought I could hold on to it, my criteria for being successful changed. Or, rather, I changed it. When reaching the bar didn't make me feel worthwhile—like it was supposed to—I had to raise it. I wasn't, after all, ready to give up on making myself worthwhile.

Perhaps you think your pursuit of money, or sex, or fame, or happiness is just that—a pursuit of money, or sex, or fame, or happiness—but if that were the case, would you still be looking? I am proposing that if you seek anything at all, you seek to know, to prove, if only to yourself, that you are once and for all good enough. You can, as you may well know, create a picture-perfect life. You can win the admiration of others and even lead them to believe that you have found the secret that eludes *them*. You will have the same doubts that they have, though, the same sense of inferiority and vulnerability, the same fear that there is something innately wrong with you—until, that is, you finally invalidate the fear, the lie, that you must *do* something to prove your worth.

At some point you will realize—whether you say it out loud or not—that there is not enough money, good looks, education, or accomplishment to make you feel the way you had hoped to feel: good enough. Society teaches us to find esteem outside of ourselves, and because we *all* learn from society, we indeed do get esteem from others by racking up what can be quantified—going to a good school, earning a lot of money, living in a prestigious neighborhood, having great children. But we cannot get *self*-esteem by racking up more money, prestige, or children. The only way to experience self-esteem, or self-verification, is to get to know yourself and *then* be yourself. You have to align your choices and behavior with who you are inside—your values, your essence, your truth, your conscience, your higher self, your whatever you prefer to call it. And you can only align with your essence, and thus find self-esteem, after you *know* your essence.

Then you have a foundation to build on. With that foundation, you can move beyond self-esteem to what gives life meaning, without the fear and the distractions that stem from ego. You can immerse yourself in beauty, revel in peace, jump up and down like a child, and love like a saint. You can get richer, better looking, wiser, kinder, and more likable with greater ease, not to prove your success or your goodness, but to simply be who you are. You can read a book, get a haircut, buy a house, get dressed, stay home, or go out without trying to substantiate your position or your worth. You can be free to follow your bliss, to find and utilize your talents. You can be you! You can be happy. *You can manifest love, which is everything good untainted by fear.* You can be more successful *and* more loving than you ever could have imagined being. You can be one with love, with life, with God.

Why, then, do we have so few saints, or enlightened gurus, or just genuinely happy people? Our biggest challenge lies in letting go of our security blanket to uncover our essence. As long as we cling to that which we have woven to mask our feelings of inferiority and win approval, we cannot see our goodness. We cannot get to know and align with our goodness. Our universal fear of rejection, which used to keep us alive, keeps us teetering. We cannot amass enough "success" to stop our pursuit of more; and as long as we're still trying to, we cannot find our innate goodness either.

You may be thinking, "What fear of rejection? I'm not afraid." Maybe you're not. There's an easy way to find out. Do you feel any negative or self-defeating emotions, such as embarrassment, shame, anger, superiority, guilt, self-pity, regret, or jealousy? They are all rooted in fear, and all of your fears can be traced to the ultimate fear that you are somehow inferior, tainted, or not good enough. You can invalidate it!

About the time I turned forty, I landed myself in my worst nightmare. When I climbed out of it a stronger person, I realized that my climb—not my fall—defined me. I was free to fail, without feeling like a failure! I knew that the only way to fail was to let fear paralyze me. That's when I mustered the guts to be no more and no less than who I was, regardless of the ramifications. I quit my job to write full-time (something I had been afraid to try), reduced my overhead, *and* managed to find a townhouse on the beach. I parked my desk in front of a big window to the ocean. I wrote. I jogged the beach, did cartwheels in the sand, and sat with the surf for hours. And I began to understand that all of my fears (and negative emotion) stemmed from the ultimate fear—yours and mine—of not being good enough. I risked nothing that I hadn't already given up on, by peering beneath the security blanket. Then I realized that I had covered up what was sacred with what was acceptable. I began to expose myself … and sharing my authentic self was part of the process of getting to know and love all of my parts. I was happier than my former frame of reference would have allowed me to imagine . . . and, through my writing and speaking, I had the privilege of helping others know and love themselves.

I will put what I know as the truth out there—reinforcing it with sentiments from some of the most revered thinkers and peacemakers of all time—and I will trust the truth to resonate with the truth written on your heart. Like your goodness, it is ever with you.

Part One

The Lie That We Are Not Good Enough as We Are

SEEK NOT GOOD FROM WITHOUT;
SEEK IT FROM WITHIN YOURSELVES,
OR YOU WILL NEVER FIND IT.

—EPICTETUS

I JOIN EPICTETUS, albeit about two thousand years later, in encouraging you to look for your goodness in the only place you can find it—within. To believe that you are not good enough as you are is to believe a lie. To try to create or earn goodness is to deny the sacred within and lose sight of it. But in the face of inevitable rejection, we respond immediately as if our survival depended on it . . . and, thus, believe a lie and lose sight of our goodness.

As human beings, we want to be accepted. Of course, we do—but we also have a *fundamental motivation* to be accepted (Baumeister and Leary 1995). We are driven to connect with others, because there was a time in our history when being solitary meant being a meal. With no scary claws or teeth, the clan was our protection. Rejection pointed to a problem that needed our attention, and our survival depended on how sensitive and responsive we were.

So from the time we were first corrected as children, we got the message that something was wrong—not with our caretaker, but with us. When our behavior, which we were too young to distinguish from ourselves, was deemed unacceptable, we felt unacceptable. We didn't know that our cries disturbed the peace, or that the electrical outlet was dangerous, or that public nudity was unacceptable. We got the message that to be a "good boy" or a "good girl," we had to sit still and be quiet with our pants on. We

3

found it impossible to conform, which left us to endure the guilt of "bad" and the burden of trying to perform better.

Supporting the notion that there is something wrong with us is the uniquely human awareness of paradise lost, which causes us to feel separate and incomplete. It, too, starts early, when we first realize that we are separate from our mothers. And in time, we develop an awareness of our nakedness and mortality.

Like those who have gone before us, we look for the how and why of our existence, and an explanation for good and evil, life and death, blessing and curse, but mostly we accept what has been handed down to us. Man has conjured up gods—both just and unjust—to account for the mysterious, that which we can neither control nor understand. Perhaps we have even wanted to blame our choices and our inherent struggle in making them on a villain; virtually every religion has one. However, once we have realized our innate goodness, by seeking it within ourselves, we need no scapegoat or "salvation." We recognize our sameness and know our oneness with the creator and the created. But in the interim, we pursue "happiness"—which only comes as a byproduct of self-verification—outside of ourselves, in what proves to be indulgence. King Solomon called it vanity (Ecclesiastes 1:2).

CHAPTER ONE

Where the Lie Came From and Why We Bought It

> TO BE A HUMAN BEING MEANS TO
> POSSESS A FEELING OF INFERIORITY WHICH
> CONSTANTLY PRESSES TOWARDS ITS OWN CONQUEST.
> THE GREATER THE FEELING OF INFERIORITY THAT
> HAS BEEN EXPERIENCED, THE MORE POWERFUL IS THE
> URGE FOR CONQUEST AND THE MORE VIOLENT
> THE EMOTIONAL AGITATION.
>
> —ALFRED ADLER

THE LONG CURLS dangled as Mom removed the sponge rollers and clipped a pink barrette to one side. Then, with a quick pat on the butt, I was off to school for picture day.

At the sound of the bell, we ran to line up behind Mrs. Davis. I wish she could have heard what Gail Reece said. I was standing right behind her—the tallest girl in first grade, and second and third and fourth—when she said my dress was ugly. Too shy to

5

say anything and too scared to cry, I cupped my disquieted insides until I got home. The school bus had scarcely stopped when I let the tears go and ran to Mom. She told me not to worry about it. She said it was a pretty pink dress, and that maybe Gail was just jealous of me. I realize now that Mom was saying not to personalize Gail's comments—great advice. It didn't break through my existing beliefs, though. Mom had already spent six years teaching me to worry about what other people thought. I was compelled—whether I realized it or not—to worry about what Gail and everybody else thought of me and my dress! So, I put on a strong little face and tried to be prettier, smarter, and "nicer." People—taller and "meaner" people—were watching. God was watching.

I know Mom wanted me to feel good about myself but, like most parents, she sent mixed messages. And I latched on to the negative. Her words haunted me. "What will people think?" "Please, act like you have some manners." "Our house is every bit as nice as theirs." It seemed as though she was trying to help me hide something or convince me of something that might not be apparent—maybe because it wasn't true. I had no inkling then that we had evolved over 150,000 years and that natural selection favored those with strong social connections! They were more apt to survive, reproduce, and raise their children to do likewise (Kurzban and Leary 2001). My mother was just trying to protect me and, on some level, herself.

I felt both my mom's regret and her hope. I was perceptive enough to realize that she wanted more for me and for herself, and I didn't want to let her down. I would keep our secrets safe. I would not talk about my dad's drinking, or her yelling and throwing him and his clothes out on some of those dark nights. I would sit still and stay clean. I would try to act normal, like nothing was wrong with us, but I would believe there was. And I resolved to do *something* to overcome the black marks.

Some children get the message that they can't—that there *is* no way for them to overcome the black marks. If they learn that being good enough means living with both parents, or growing up on the other side of town, or being a different color, then the best they can hope for is to build a good facade. They might build what turns out to be an elaborate system of defense mechanisms to protect themselves and keep others at arm's length from the truth. Then, they might spend their lives in fear of being found out. If this is all too familiar, maybe it's because you've done the same thing while working—year after year—on *something* to overcome your own black marks. What *I* decided was normal or good enough was an ideal that existed only in fairy tales. I would be painfully private and strong (to appear as normal as possible) as I struggled toward perfection—the kind you only get when you walk off into the sunset at "The End." And that's not a real option, for any of us, even for the most "blessed" or "gifted." Take Dante, for example.

With an IQ of 170, a passion for philosophy, and a wit that can impale adults more than three times his twelve years of age, Dante struggles with self-esteem. And his parents worry that he could suffer from depression, because of a fixation with being perfect.

He attends a highly selective private school with many gifted children, yet its teachers still find Dante intimidating—quick to pick holes in any illogical argument or lack of knowledge. The eminent child psychologist who assessed him explained that he had a complex and intriguing personality and a fantastic wit, but "somehow had the feeling of not being quite good enough."

We all have a story, a different story, with the same message, the same fear that something is wrong with us.

"Often, just telling people that others feel neutrally about them will be perceived as rejection. That's one thing that's been amazing to me—very small doses of rejection elicit strong emotional reactions. It shows how powerful this motive [to be socially accepted] is," says Mark Leary, a professor of psychology and neuroscience at Duke University, whose research focuses on how people's behavior and emotions are affected by their concerns about others' impressions, evaluations, and acceptance of them.

The Message That We Are Not Good Enough— From the Voice of Authority

From the time we understand the word "no," we begin to feed the notion that something is wrong with us that needs to be corrected. We start to venture off, and somebody says, "No." We reach for something that catches our eye, and somebody says—or even screams—no. We don't immediately cave. We think when somebody says "no," we can do it anyway, maybe just as soon as they turn their head again! Most of us try—until we learn the voice of authority, the authority being the one who can slap our hand, or withhold cookies, or approval, or love.

"The average child hears 432 negative statements per day to only 32 positive statements," says Jack Canfield, a self-esteem expert.

When our behavior, which we are unable to distinguish from ourselves, is rejected, we feel rejected. We do not understand *what* is wrong with us, only that something is. Even when we eventually understand that Daddy is trying to protect us, the message is one of fear. There is something to be afraid of; and we are not up to the task of managing it on our own. If we venture off, we risk destruction and rejection. The alternative is to succumb to fear.

We have all seen children stifled by fear, trying desperately to hold back the tears, because even *the tears* are rejected. We have also seen children who seem carefree and happy, children who are delighted by both caterpillars and butterflies. There is nothing as pure as a child who is still innocent of prejudice. Nonetheless, we are compelled to protect and socialize children, and in doing so, we inevitably taint them in some way. Please stay with me—I can hear the objections. Yes, many children grow up in "loving" homes. I did.

"Even if you were fortunate enough to grow up in a safe, nurturing environment, you still bear invisible scars from childhood, because from the very moment you were born you were a complex, dependent creature with a never-ending cycle of needs. Freud correctly labeled us 'insatiable beings.' And no parents, no matter how devoted, are able to respond perfectly to all of these changing needs," says Harville Hendrix in his bestselling *Getting the Love You Want*. Hendrix goes on to share how he and his wife, despite their best intentions, didn't meet all of their daughter's needs because they were too tired or distracted or unwittingly passed on their own childhood wounds. Even if we were to succeed in being more loving parents than Hendrix and his wife (one of the most knowledgeable and loving couples I can imagine), there is still, as they point out, the strange dog or slip in the pool that leads to fear.

We can't keep children from getting scared anymore than we can keep them from falling. We *can* be there for them. We *can* teach them not to personalize rejection *and* not to worry about what other people think. And, we can give them a path back to paradise, to peace on the other side of the inevitable bruised butt and heart.

"I would not give a fig for the simplicity this side of complexity, but I would give my life for the simplicity on the other side of complexity," said Oliver Wendell Holmes. And that is what we are destined to find, a paradise worthy of the bruises, a paradise made possible by the bruises.

A dear man who attended one of my workshops shared his first memory of his mother: when he looked up and saw his mother standing in the doorway, he was sitting on the kitchen floor amid the scattered pots and pans that he had pulled from the cabinets. She shook her head and smiled, making a sweet sound as she pursed her lips together. Then she sat on the floor with him.

Together, they put the pots and pans away. Too young to remember any words, he remembers his mother's acceptance, and he conveyed it with the bright-eyed enthusiasm of a toddler and the peaceful knowing of a sixty-year-old man!

Many of us—even from loving parents—learn *not* to make a mess. We learn not to fidget or talk too much. We learn not to interrupt adults or bother them with things that are "unimportant." We learn not to talk back and not to hit back. We learn not to be stingy and not to hold a grudge. We learn to love God and others but not really . . . unless we also learn to love ourselves. We can't truly love anybody else until we do. The often misused commandment says, "Love your neighbor *as* you love yourself."

As long as we feel unlovable, we don't want to believe that others *are* lovable. We are motivated to find fault with them rather than accept them as they are and love them unconditionally (which is the only way to truly love somebody). We are afraid that they won't reciprocate. And if we withhold no part of ourselves and love them, the decidedly lovable, with no qualifiers, and they still don't love us, then what? That would confirm the lie, our worst fear, that we are unlovable.

Even parents can find themselves hurting when their children don't appreciate or reciprocate love. Parents don't just worry about what their children think, though. As long as their insecurity rules, they also worry about what others think—of both them and their children. And what most impresses others is not necessarily what is most loving. Conflicted intentions—to love and to gain approval—work against each other and render us ineffective at any age. We cannot fully love somebody, anybody, while feeling torn. Love is wholehearted. So parents often give children a false concept of what love is, while passing on their insecurity as part of it.

Many of us learn that we are unworthy—even of this false concept of love. No problem . . . Mommy and Daddy love us, even if we *are* bad! And what about everybody else? To move beyond our badness to be good enough, we must obey the rules, meet the standards, present ourselves as pretty or handsome, earn good grades, perform well in games or sports. The belief that we must *do* something to measure up leaves us striving. However, we cannot feel good if our goodness is based on meeting certain criteria, just as we cannot feel loved if being loved is based on meeting certain criteria. As children, we are not yet able to reason this out. Besides, our parents are the authorities. They are the trusted ones. Our well-being hangs on their knowing what they're doing. We're not ready to question their competence (a word we've yet to learn).

When baby elephants are born in the circus, the trainers use heavy chains to get the desired response. In time, they use a lighter chain and, eventually, an even lighter rope. The elephants grow bigger and more powerful, but they continue to respond to the rope as they did to the heavy chain. Although they could almost effortlessly break free, they *believe* the rope is strong enough to control them.

Most of us learn to heed "no," particularly when it comes from the voice of authority—a caretaker (usually a parent), a teacher, or the adult in charge. We learn that, "No means no." And we can turn each "no" into a belief, a chain, that disempowers us—and we continue to respond to those chains long after we are mature enough to free ourselves. We lose awareness of our true nature and believe that our goodness is contingent on meeting the criteria set out by the authority. We hear things like, "Be good now, stay right here, and be quiet." We get the message that what we would do instinctively is unacceptable. We learn, often from the people we depend upon for survival, not to trust ourselves! We feel guilty not just for running or playing, but for wanting to. We feel guilty for being who we naturally are . . . and we begin to screen what we show of ourselves. And, to the degree that we repress parts of ourselves, we lose our awareness of them. So, we cannot feel whole (read: good).

Pam's story, as shared with me during a one-on-one consultation, might remind you of one of your own. Pam began wearing eyeglasses as a very young child, maybe when she was three. And because her mother was wary of her losing the glasses, she almost constantly warned Pam of what would happen if she did. "Stay here and hold on to your glasses," she would tell her little girl, "because if you wander off and lose them, you won't be able to find your way back to me again." This instilled such a fear in Pam that she was terrified of taking the glasses off. She relied on them and her mother more than she needed to. She was in her thirties when she met with me and finally realized that she had been afraid all those years "to take the glasses off" or stray from her mother. And as long as she stayed close and looked through the "glasses," she saw things through her mother's eyes of fear. She had been afraid of losing both the glasses and her mother, and as a result, she had lost her own eyes, her own view, her own judgment. Once she realized what had happened, she saw things through new eyes. She also realized that they were "good" eyes.

All of our parts are good, but many of us got the message that some of them—particularly our genitals—are taboo. In the movie *The Good Mother,* a little girl is removed from her very loving home after being allowed to touch a penis. And despite the sexual education now available for children—which the "good mother" used—some parents still teach their children that it is inappropriate to touch a penis, even if that penis is just as much a part of their own body as their arm or their ear (and a more curious part, at that). What if those of us who grew up without the books had been taught that it was okay to touch a penis or those female parts that even now I can't think of comfortable names for? What if we had grown up knowing it was okay to talk about our genitals? Wouldn't we have healthier bodies with more awareness of them? Wouldn't we have healthier psyches without the repressed sexual feelings, without the shame and the guilt? Wouldn't we be more sexually discerning and satisfied?

And our repressed feelings and shame, as we've seen, are not restricted to our sexuality. We may learn to keep our tears to ourselves—until we grow up and marry somebody, somebody who screams out desperately to know what we are feeling. We may learn to keep our anger in—until we literally explode. Ideally, children are taught to recognize their emotions and understand and appreciate them, to learn from them. Our emotions always have something important to teach us. The idea is not to repress the fear—or the emotions that stem from it—but to confront it. Only then can we realize that we don't have anything to be afraid of. But adults can't teach children what they haven't learned. Hence, we grow up judging ourselves based on what often unhealthy authority figures tell us is appropriate to do, and feel, and think, and be, and when we judge ourselves, we also feel judged by others.

Some of the messages come in a certain look or a "shhh." My mother used to make a gesture with her two index fingers that meant "shame on you." We don't need words to feel shamed or stifled. Sometimes we get the message that there is something to be kept undercover, without ever understanding exactly what. It is, after all, to be kept quiet. And we shy away from asking, "Exactly what is wrong with me?" Other messages come through the absence of attention. What does it tell a child when Grandpa is always too busy to answer his questions, or Grandma has time for baby brother but not for her? The new bike seems like a consolation prize when there is nobody there to watch him ride it. Unworthiness can be passed on by anybody in a position of authority—without words or even awareness.

Children are optimistic, though. They find hope, even when there is none. They latch on to whatever contingency they can find to make themselves good enough. It may be holding on to their glasses or retreating quietly to their room to read. It may be making a fist and bullying other children. It may be staying clean and "pretty."

The Criteria to *Make* Ourselves Good Enough

APPEARANCE

Virtually all of us learn about appearance. Some of the earliest remarks about our bald heads or bowlegs slip by us, but without our parents even realizing it, we learn that we look better when we get dressed and comb our hair. And even then, it seems somebody wants to smooth out the rough edges for us, before we are exposed to the clerk at the grocery store or, God forbid, Aunt Harriett. Particularly if you still do the smoothing for a child (or a spouse), you might be thinking, "But don't we look better when we comb our hair?" Maybe, but who can be objective? My husband envisions me with long gray hair and himself with a beard and a straw hat; we're in a garden and we live in a bungalow on stilts. Do we still comb our hair? I think so, but not because of ego or perception. For now, we want to share what we've learned about love; and we live in a society in which perception matters. But doesn't the mere idea of letting that go—entirely—feel liberating?

I learned from my little brothers that I had nostrils like a pig's. It took a plastic surgeon, when I was twenty-nine, to tell me that ideally a woman's nose is turned up. And, as though he were the new authority, I believed him. Funny, though, I don't remember asking him about how wide my nostrils were. Maybe I was afraid *that* was a problem he couldn't fix!

There is almost an epidemic in young girls—models, pageant queens, dancers, and wannabes—who are obsessed with their appearance. We're giving them the message that appearance is more important than it is. They cling to it, color it, tweak it, trim it, firm it, and take pride in it . . . as though it has the power to make them something that they are not—good enough! And let's not fool ourselves—this misplaced priority factors into the life of virtually every little girl, diverting her attention from what's inside!

EDUCATION

Shortly after we learn about appearance, we learn about education or grades. My goal was to get an "A" with as little effort as possible. I still remember sitting down with my middle school counselor when I landed in an English class full of the brainy kids. When I asked Mr. Daley to transfer me, he said I would have to try a little harder to get an "A" where I was, and that I would only try as hard as I had to. Those words pointed to something I hadn't seen—and my behavior would bring them to mind over and over again in the coming years. But it was *many* years later before I would realize that Mr. Daley didn't just want me to try harder; he wanted me to *learn* more. As silly as it sounds, that wasn't in my equation. When I studied for a test, it was to get an "A." Now when I learn something, it's because I want to apply it—not use it for a grade, or stockpile it.

Education is not about a grade or a degree or amassing more; it's about learning something that enhances our life and the lives of those around us. I remember my friend Belinda Grady, from the same small Midwestern school, talking about college while we were still in fifth grade. Her sisters were already attending college, and although her parents had more children than money, college was assumed. She didn't just earn an "A," she understood what was in the books. I wrote book reports from back covers; she learned what was inside. I don't know if she was taught the importance of education in following your dreams or making a positive difference or if she was taught that to be good enough, she had to go to college, which meant learning as much as she could to win a scholarship. When I was sixteen and wanted to get married, my mom insisted that I finish high school; my dad said, "Jan-Jan's smart enough already." Of course, I wasn't. I just knew how to get an "A" and how to pretend like nothing was wrong. Ironically, both of my parents were trying to teach me to survive—they had learned different methods of doing it.

SPORTS

Some kids were better at hitting home runs—and some of them seemed to overemphasize physical strength and coordination. I was the last one picked for softball; I learned what it felt like to be the lone kid standing in the middle of the field, looking in both directions to see which team would end up with me so I could start walking. But in families where athletic ability is expected, or even demanded, sports can be serious business. You might have to perform the way Dad did, or almost did, to be good enough. While many parents cheer their children on from the sidelines, if you have survived the rigors of Little League, you have likely seen those parents who curse the umps and the coaches. Surely, these parents are not upset about the game itself. It is more than a game to them; it is what makes their child—and perhaps them—good enough. And, therefore, it is to the child what makes him good enough—or not good enough.

POSSESSIONS

Then there are children who learn that being good enough means living in a house on the lake or driving a new car. They judge others—and themselves—based on money, or class, or both. They feel superior to some; they feel inferior to others. Somebody always has more . . . and the pressure to get it starts early. Conversely, parents can teach their children that rich people are arrogant or selfish or on their way to hell! These children—whether they realize it or not—can grow up pressured to be both good enough and poor enough.

ANOTHER KIND OF PRESSURE

And there is another kind of pressure: some children are not pushed by their parents to be "good." They get the message that they are a burden. Rather than try to measure up, they try to survive, mostly on their own. They try not to get in the way or demand too much time or money. Both are in short supply. Their stories don't get much attention, unless they beat the odds through the help of a family member or teacher or "angel."

TRUE WORTH

Every child is a miracle in progress. In Oprah Winfrey's own words, "I came to live with my grandmother because I was a child born out of wedlock, and my mother moved to the North. . . . By the time I was three, I was reciting speeches in the church. And they'd put me up on the program, and they would say, 'And Little Mistress Winfrey will render a recitation,' and I would do 'Jesus rose on Easter Day, Hallelujah, Hallelujah, all the angels did proclaim.' And all the sisters sitting in the front row would fan themselves and turn to my grandmother and say, 'Ida Mae, this child is gifted.' And I heard that enough that I started to believe it."

"When those you respect think you can, YOU think you can. [Children] rise or fall to the level of expectation of their teachers. When teachers believe in students, students believe in themselves" (James Raffini 1993). A recent article in the *New York Times* questioned whether children were now getting too much praise. An "inflated ego" to come crumbling down is not the goal; self-esteem is. Like love, praise at its best is guided by knowledge and rooted in truth; it's not loosely thrown out with no foundation. With keen discernment, we internalize what parents and teachers *believe* about us—not necessarily what they say. Unfortunately, their beliefs often fall short of their hopes for us, increasing the chances that we'll disappoint them. And even when they believe we can meet whatever criteria they've laid out, it may be ill-defined and difficult to hold on to.

A young Japanese man explained to me that when he was a

young boy, he worked very hard to attend a prestigious middle school. He studied . . . and studied . . . and studied. Once he was accepted by the school, he thought everything would be okay. But when he entered the school, he got lost among all the other over-achievers, many of whom were "superior." He no longer felt "special." Acceptance by the school seemed to rob him of the one thing he thought he had—academic standing. He ate himself to obesity and developed a nervous twitch. People looked at him like he was a freak, while his family insisted that he should control himself. As a young adolescent, he had already worked diligently for the hope of approval—and lost it. Now in the United States, a decade later, he continued to feel like a misfit. He wanted love and intimacy with a woman. Instead, he had sex that felt shame-ful, because he was too afraid to open up and disclose himself. As he communicated his story during a weekend retreat, each member of the group felt his pain as he pressed on and continued shar-ing. I have never seen a more earnest face or felt a more resolved spirit.

It brought to mind my own misguided tenacity. I remembered dating a young cardiologist who had graduated from Yale; his father was chief of staff at a hospital, and his brother and sister were also doctors. I felt that maybe he was enough to finally make me "okay." As I told my mother about him, she said that his family would probably never allow him to marry me because he was Jewish. I felt shame in that moment—it seemed like what she was really saying is that they couldn't possibly find me suitable (read: good enough) for their son. My mom wanted me to be all

I could be, but I think she saw limits that would keep me from being good enough in the eyes of others. And I think she saw those limits as stopping me. And although I could also see them and feel them, I couldn't let them stop me. I wanted to feel and be good enough . . . not just for me but for her and my father. They had virtually spent themselves on their six children, and I wanted to give them a good return. Perhaps I wanted to be worthy of their investment.

Parents can easily overlook the role their own self-esteem plays in the self-esteem of their children. No matter how much good they see in their children, they also see themselves in there. And if *they* still feel inadequate, they instinctively defend their offspring; even when there is no rejection or attack, they anticipate it. They fear that their children lack something, that they don't quite measure up . . . that they require a defense. But if Dad introduces a son who could have gone all the way if he'd stayed in school, he sells both of them short. And we all know parents who defend their children as though they can do no wrong. It is not because they really think their children are perfect; it is because they are scared to death to look at the "flaws" or let others see them. They prefer to maintain a facade, no matter how difficult or obvious or painful. Sadly, the pain is often beneath the surface of consciousness—perhaps masked by anger or shyness or busyness.

My mom is an intelligent and intuitive woman, but I wonder if I felt more of her pain than she allowed herself to feel. When the pain of growing up seemed more than I could bare, I sought God's help. And with a child's faith, I found it. But the dogma (as I knew it) of my Assembly of God church—oddly enough—in some ways kept me from knowing the God of unconditional love I now know.

For Many, Religious Doctrine Validates the Message of Not Being Good Enough

From the proverbial beginning—of man as we know him—we looked to the gods as a source of both reward and punishment. Thunder sent the message that the gods were angry with us, and when cold weather and drought killed off our crops, surely we were being punished from on high. We would chant and dance, burn offerings, and mutilate our bodies to make amends. And we are still trying to measure up and find favor.

On a recent trip to China, in a Buddhist monastery, I looked on as a young nun with a shaved head did a set of calisthenics until she was exhausted, only to do another set, another, and another, and another. If there was any joy or peace to be found in her ritual, it did not show on her forlorn face. Maybe she was just in the zone . . . or doing her best to get there. Either way, I deeply respect her effort. And we need not go to China to find worshippers making valiant effort. Some of our Catholic priests have cut off their sexuality and found themselves preying on the innocence and trust of youth, only to feel more inadequate and shameful for having done so. I don't seek to condemn them or anybody else. I seek to help people find their goodness, rather than try to earn it.

For many of us, the notion that we are not good enough is validated by the Christian doctrine that we are born sinners and drawn to sin, even after forgiveness, because of our sinful—or what is sadly labeled human—nature. In Buddhism, there is no punishment, but there is karma and no escaping an evil deed—"not in the sky, nor in the midst of the sea, nor yet in the clefts of the mountains," says the Dhammapada. In Islam, there is the belief that we are prone to evil and that even the prophets don't absolve themselves of blame. In Judaism, there can be a burden of ritual and atonement. In Confucianism, merit can only be used to help one's ancestors. But I think the weight of religion is largely based on misinterpretation. Jesus, for example, did not offer a long list of dos and don'ts; he demonstrated love. He said *we* could fulfill the commandments by doing the same. And Buddha said, "The wise man no longer concerns himself with this or that system (or philosophy), he neither prides nor deceives himself. He goes along his independent way." Muhammad said, "Learn to know thyself. Who knows himself, knows his lord."

Every great teacher teaches that we can somehow overcome our separateness to know oneness with the light. That is, in fact, the goal of every major religion. And we accomplish that goal by recognizing our innate goodness or the divine spirit within. We were never really separate; we only perceived ourselves to be separate. But until we recognize our goodness and reconcile it with the source of all goodness, we *feel* separate.

And separate is exactly how I felt growing up. I knew God well enough to want to be like him; and without realizing it, I had the same yearning that we all have to return to paradise. I had been taught a long list of dos and don'ts, though, and I did not have to break the rules to feel guilty. I only had to think about breaking them because I had learned that "Everyone who looks at a woman with lust for her has already committed adultery with her in his heart" (Matthew 5:28). But I had also been taught that "All things are possible to him who believes" (Mark 9:23). And I had the faith of a child. Still, it is no wonder that I felt so much weight as a six-year-old and an eight-year-old and a fourteen-year-old. I inevitably fell short of my goal, my idea of the perfection possible through Jesus Christ, if I could only believe . . . enough. I was twenty-seven, I had been married, and divorced, I was living in a house I had built, and I was working for a Fortune 500 company before I had the guts to—very quietly in the privacy of my own living room with a refreshingly intellectual minister—question what I had been taught.

"Ma" Ferguson, the first female governor of Texas, in 1925, is quoted as saying, "If the King's English was good enough for Jesus, it's good enough for me!"

WE LET GO OF SOME OF THE FALSE MESSAGES

It is rather amazing when you think about what we are still afraid to question, but it is not amazing that we believed it as children. What else could we do? We were in no position to launch our own theories, just as we were in no position to start off on our own and set up housekeeping. Although, I suppose most of us speculated about how one could survive in the belly of a big fish for three days, just as we took a shot at bundling a few things together and running away (once I got as far as the backseat of the family car, with a Hostess cherry pie and my pajamas).

We didn't just buy into the idea that we were innately bad, or flawed, or in need of salvation. Most of us also bought into the idea that there was a fat, jolly man in a red suit who dropped down every chimney on Christmas Eve, while his reindeer waited with his sleigh full of toys. Believing in Santa Claus was believing in Christmas. Of course, we *wanted* to believe. And the naughty-and-nice list seemed a natural part of the system of reward and punishment. Then there was the Tooth Fairy who slipped through the window and under our pillow (even when we'd dropped our tooth down the drain). We were given permission to stop believing in some of the myths—the ones our authority figures weren't still clinging to.

"We stop believing in Santa Claus, but we do not stop loving him," says Glenn Grace, one of my favorite psychologists. If we can stop believing in Santa Claus without betraying him, we can, without betraying God, stop believing that Eve, upon tasting the fruit of the tree of the knowledge of good and evil, doomed the human race to sin. We can find and hold the truth dear without holding on, for fear of judgment, to a myth as though it were intended to be taken literally. But that's tough to pull off when we are six, or eight, or even twenty-eight, when our authority figures still believe.

So we continue to believe the lie that there is something wrong with us and that to be good enough we must find the right hoops to jump through. We reach for them, lose them, and reach for them again and again. We struggle to reconcile the system of hoops with what we can reach or what we can hope to reach. It doesn't matter how well we do, though, because as long as our goodness is contingent on meeting certain criteria, we don't feel *truly* good. We know fleeting moments of goodness, but we often wear a mask that both isolates us and threatens to expose us.

Others Reinforce the Message of Not Good Enough

We are not alone. We are surrounded by peers who are also trying to feel good about themselves—too often by making us look bad. As long as children have insecurities, they will shoot holes in other children in an effort to feel better about themselves. It is easy to see why Gail Reece told me my little pink dress was ugly. I didn't point to shortcomings out loud, but I found it reassuring that the smart girl wasn't rich, and the rich girl wasn't that pretty. For years, I took consolation in Scott Thompson choosing me over Patty Brolin, who lived on the river and had the second-highest IQ in our fifth-grade class and was the first to wear bell-bottoms. Somehow it made my growing list of flaws easier to bear—even ignore, on occasion.

We are also surrounded by the insecure parents of our peers, all of whom have a vested interest in making their own children look good, which means stretching the truth to make them look better than we do and make us look worse than we *are*. When something bad happens, these parents blame the "bad" child in the neighborhood or the school or the church . . . and they just might label our parents "bad" as well. With that, the hole we find ourselves in gets a little deeper.

And then there are well-meaning family members and "friends" who have their say—or take their shots. I can still see the robust wife of a friend of my father's clamoring at our kitchen table. While she sat there, my sister walked through the kitchen carrying her bra from the laundry room. This woman burst into laughter and said, "What could she possibly need a bra for?" Younger and less developed than my sister, I was already self-conscious. I stayed in my bedroom until she was gone and I felt safe to come out and defend my sister (and, thus, myself), which sounded like, "She's just a fat loudmouth."

If family and friends didn't tell us what was wrong with us, there were myriad for-profit businesses pointing to our inadequacies, while competing for our parents' money to fix them. If somehow we didn't notice that extra space between our teeth—and the other kids didn't point it out—the billboards for braces would surely get our attention. We could hardly miss the campaigns for sneakers. And doesn't every *lovable* little girl have a Barbie doll and new bell-bottoms?

Lost Paradise Also Supports the Message

Supporting the message that we are not good enough is the uniquely human awareness of a lost paradise, of our nakedness and mortality, which causes us to feel separate and incomplete. However vague or distant, we have an awareness of what once was—before being forced from paradise, or the womb, as the case may be. While still connected to our lifeline, our needs were seamlessly met before we had any knowledge of them. We had no need to seek food, water, or shelter. We had nothing to flee, no one to protect ourselves from. We had nothing to fear. We made no distinction between ourselves and our mothers; we made no distinction between ourselves and all that is. We knew only peace and oneness. But perhaps we knew these things with no realization of what they were. Nonetheless, many scholars agree with the pioneer thinking of Otto Rank that our unconscious perpetually feeds a lifelong desire to return to our paradise lost. "So every pleasure has as its final aim the re-establishment of the intrauterine primal pleasure," said Rank.

We are unlikely to consciously *face* our separateness, though, until we begin to realize our innate goodness and feel worthy of reconciliation. Only then can we recognize our sameness with all that is; only then can we know our oneness with the creator and the created. Until then, we are sensitive to what reinforces the lie that something is wrong with us, and we feel compelled to correct what is wrong. We are left wanting. We are left working to prove our worth by meeting whatever criteria has been laid out.

CHAPTER TWO

Trying to Meet the Criteria for Good Enough

> IF A MAN DOES NOT KEEP PACE WITH
> HIS COMPANIONS, PERHAPS IT IS BECAUSE HE HEARS
> A DIFFERENT DRUMMER. LET HIM STEP TO
> THE MUSIC WHICH HE HEARS, HOWEVER
> MEASURED OR FAR AWAY.
>
> —HENRY DAVID THOREAU

WE INEVITABLY FEEL pushed to meet the criteria on which our goodness is contingent. We are driven to find a way to fit in and prove that we are worthwhile, and we have an innate longing to align with our essence and return to paradise. To *ignore* the criteria would be to give up.

We keep trying. We plod on, and on, and on—even in the face of dead ends. Often marked "success" or "pleasure," the paths to "happiness" are well trodden by people who appear to be happy—or at least without apparent reason for their unhappiness.

Despite our efforts, and despite the fact that we may appear to others as having no reason for *our* unhappiness, we fall short. The problem is that the criteria laid out to make us good enough is not our music. And in trying to meet the criteria, we may stray so far from our music that we can faintly hear it. But the music still sounds.

Fear Shields Us from the Truth

The same people who push us may also hold us back out of fear. On top of that, we have our own fears—of both failure and success. Fear is *the only thing* that holds us back, trips us up, or makes us fight, run away, or settle for less than what we want. And it is the only thing that keeps us from looking within to realize that we are innately good, with no qualifiers.

I still remember the words from one of my niece's school programs, "What would you choose if you couldn't fail?" I sat there watching the students' little faces beam with enthusiasm and faith. I listened to their mostly well-rehearsed lines; my niece's, "There are infinite possibilities in little beginnings," is etched in my memory. Their faces, their words, their songs all said, "You can do anything." And in that moment, I believed that I could have done anything, and that belief offered me a glimpse of what I would have chosen had I not been afraid. I thought, "I could have done *anything*, and look at me." But it only took me a moment to realize that it is never, ever, ever, ever too late to answer the question, "What would you choose if you couldn't fail?"

When we answer that question, we begin to hear the music of our "distant drummer." We get a glimpse of what we would do if our parents and society had not laid out a list of expectations for us, if they, and perhaps the God we learned to fear, weren't watching and judging us. We see what we could do with our whole heart, with all of our passion, instead of the rationale imposed on us by a society that's all wrapped up in fear. We see our potential and not our limits. We see who we are!

Would I hold on to the question? Would I hold on to the belief that I could do anything, or would I walk out of the school auditorium and hug my niece, say hello to a stranger or two, feel the cool air, and forget? Would the little kids hold on to their bright-eyed enthusiasm, or would it be dampened by their parents, their teachers, their peers, their falls? We learn faith and optimism (my mom and dad taught them); we just don't learn them as well as we learn fear and doubt.

Programmed to Beware the Negative

In fairness, we are biologically programmed through thousands of years of evolution to beware of the negative, just as we are programmed to be sensitive to rejection (Leary and Downs 1995). It's a survival technique—a predator once represented a terminal threat. So the positive may sail right by us, while the negative immediately gets our attention. You've been there—rehearsing the negative, analyzing what was intended by it. How could he possibly think that all you do is complain? Or how could she stoop to attacking your mother? That one remark that triggers our insecurity can sabotage a whole weekend. And enough remarks—well rehearsed—can sabotage a whole lot of weekends. According to research by John Gottman of the Gottman Institute, couples need a minimum of five positive interactions for every one negative interaction to stay together happily.

Besides being biologically programmed to be aware of the negative and defend ourselves, we are also programmed to defend our belief that there is something wrong with us. The term "cognitive dissonance" explains the discomfort we feel when we have conflicting thoughts. We are so motivated to avoid the discomfort that we guard against what contradicts our established thinking or beliefs. As we filter incoming data, we can use what reinforces our beliefs and conveniently ignore the rest.

Some argue that the need to have "consonant cognitions," or thoughts that go together, is as strong as our need for food and shelter. In any case, when we meet with dissonant cognitions, we put up a fight—or a filter, as the case may be. Let's say that you have grown up feeling shy and awkward, like you're different and don't really fit in. And one day you overhear a coworker saying, "Oh, I don't think Janine [that's you] would want to go *there* with us." Although (1) the comment says as much about your coworkers as it does about you, (2) it could have been a compliment, and (3) you've gone out with them on other occasions and felt accepted (and even enjoyed yourself in moments of grace when you weren't worried about what everybody was thinking), you remember that one comment. It's recorded in your psyche and it plays over and over and over again, each time reinforcing your belief that you don't really fit in. There's more to it than that, though; the comment also reinforces your belief that you're inferior and somehow flawed. You don't just think that the music you hear is different; you think that it's somehow inferior.

Let me guess—you've never felt shy and awkward. How about fat and ugly—or just fat or just ugly—or short and squeaky (there's a professor in Texas who calls me the shrimp with the squeaky voice), or how about loudmouthed, dim-witted (as in you're always afraid you'll miss the punch line), outclassed, or dorky? Where did that notion come from? How often have you reinforced it? And would you have found reinforcement had you not been looking for it? You only have to feel fat or loud or outclassed if you want to. You can discard any belief that doesn't serve you—and with new beliefs come new feelings. You might be thinking, "Wait a minute, I really *am* fat." I understand—I really am short. But it's not that simple. Some people think 5'4" is short; but as near as I can tell from statistics, the average woman is about my height. Regardless, I can decide for myself what's short, and I can decide for myself what short means, what it says about me or any other person. The same thing applies to fat; only if the excess weight doesn't serve you, you can lose it (but you don't lose it to feel good about yourself; you lose it as a result of feeling good about yourself—more on that in Chapter 7).

Let's take this a step further. As part of a leadership program, I participated in SimSoc ("simulated society"). Each enrollee (maybe eighty people) was assigned one of four colors. And as we opened an envelope with our name on it, we discovered our fate—red, blue, yellow, or green. I was a red and quickly learned that all reds would be based in the copy/storage room of the Chamber of Commerce building. There we learned what it meant to be a red. I remember trying to explain to the rest of the reds that it was okay if we didn't have any jobs or food vouchers; we could be creative and find a means of earning money and surviving within the rules outlined for the society. It was then that I was sarcastically dubbed "Little Miss Sunshine."

As I recall, for two or three days, we played our roles. The memory of one lunch sticks in my mind: while the greens were upstairs with steak, baked potatoes, salads, and candelabras, we reds were served some water in a plastic jug with a loaf of bread—and somebody had apparently put their fist through the bread. About that time, the reds (successful leaders in real life) turned into "hoodlums." They stole the toilet paper, turned off the water, and so on. I and another red named Vicki tried to encourage other reds to take advantage of opportunities within the society and do something constructive. They would have none of it—they preferred to act in anger (read: fear). But Vicki and I did in fact move through the ranks to become greens. The reds thought of us as traitors and gave us a color all our own, calling us "browns." And the greens didn't really accept us, either—they were afraid we were going to get our hands on their piece of the pie.

It was absolutely amazing to me that people, including me, took it *so* seriously. It was just a game. The original roles were assigned—we did nothing to "deserve" red, green, yellow, or blue.

Yet the people seemed to take on the attitudes of the poverty-stricken, the elite snobs, the lower class, and the middle class, respectively. In real life, we also open up an envelope, if you will, with our name on it. But we can, as countless others have, reach beyond the envelope. In fact, we must often transcend the circumstances of our origins if we are to become who we really are. And I can tell you—based on my own real-life experience—that "brown" is nothing to be afraid of. At the end of the leadership program, a group produced a video redeeming those who were dubbed as traitors!

Our fear, and all of the emotions that stem from it, was *intended* to help us deal with important events. There was a time when a partner showing attention to somebody else meant there wouldn't be enough food for *our* babies. There was a time when rejection—or losing a member of your group to another group—translated into a death threat. Fear—and the prejudice, anger, greed, and jealousy that stem from it—served us when we were a more primal part of the animal kingdom. But as we embrace our knowledge of good and evil and our responsibility to care for ourselves, each other, and the planet, we are better served by love.

We must, then, be careful about what we believe and how we feel—about ourselves and others. And when we find ourselves close-minded, or perhaps even a bit opinionated or defensive, we can see it as a big red flag that suggests we're holding a lie or distorting the truth to justify what can only be destructive behavior. If it helps, we can turn that red flag into a picture of one of those close-minded people (from the other side of the proverbial aisle) who we don't want to emulate, and that just might save us from digging our heels into quicksand.

The first thing we have to do is grow up. And the same people who want us to be all we can be are afraid to let us. It is difficult to stand by and let a child learn for himself that the stove is hot, but maybe it's even more difficult to describe a hot stove to a child and effectively teach a lesson in safe behavior without allowing him to reap the consequences of unsafe behavior. And let's face it, we don't just teach children to be afraid of a hot stove; we teach them to be afraid of falling down—not just because it hurts, but because people are watching! We teach them to be afraid of what we want to keep them from—including failure and, ironically, rejection. And they can't go very far without "failure." A famous quote by Thomas Edison says, "I have not failed. I've just found 10,000 ways that won't work." We, too, can reframe failure instead of teaching children to be afraid of it.

Fear of Success

Success can be just as scary as failure. What if we don't know what to do with it? What if we lose it? Often I talk to men who are afraid to ask the good-looking woman out—not just because she might say no, but because she might say yes. Then what? If he doesn't feel worthy of the hot babe, or the studious lawyer, or the gifted artist, then how can he not be afraid of spending an evening—or a night—with her? And if he does get his arms around her, he's scared to death he's going to lose her. How could he possibly get that "lucky" again? You see, he still believes he's unworthy of her, and that's a surefire way to lose her and *prove* his belief. He may not be ready to *change* his belief, but that doesn't mean he's ready to out-and-out prove it to the world.

We can be unhappy with our situation and still find comfort in the familiar. The house may need repairs, the job may be grueling, but they are familiar. There is comfort in what we know, and fear in what we don't know—unless we believe in our ability to manage it. Then we expand our comfort zone and accelerate our growth. But if you don't believe you can hold on to the new job, you may attach more shame to getting it than to *not* getting it. If you don't believe you're one of those people who "belong" at a fancy party, you might want to save yourself the embarrassment of showing up. If you don't believe you can invest money wisely, you might hide what you have under the mattress and sit in your little house and wait for inflation.

With or without realizing it, we stifle our dreams—with fear. We might rationalize that our dreams were unrealistic and settle for "real life." We might erect walls that keep us in little boxes— and still wonder why we never get ahead. We might bemoan our circumstances and find others to blame for our mediocrity. We might beat ourselves up—if only privately—for failing, for missing opportunities, for screwing up over and over again. But we can't kill our dreams, because we can't kill love.

We plod on, maybe we try harder, and maybe we exhaust ourselves—not so much because the work is difficult, but because it is discouraging. Work, even suffering, with a purpose is gratifying.

"In some way, suffering ceases to be suffering at the moment it finds a meaning," said Viktor Frankl, a Holocaust survivor and psychoanalyst. We grow weary of trying when we can see no meaning and no light, particularly when we labor alone. But we make some headway and see glimpses of light; we know success—even if not at the level we could know it, even if not as well as failure.

We persevere; maybe we reach one goal, then another, and another. Still, it never quite feels the way we imagined it would, at least not for very long. We might enter the top-notch school feeling insecure. We might accept the promotion with great anticipation, only to realize that the title, the pay, and the windowed office don't change who we are. No matter how many people believe in us, if we still have our doubts, we can feel like frauds.

I remember my surprise when I attended my first professional seminar as a human resources manager. I was doing everything right. I expected to learn that the real professionals knew something I didn't. I was relieved to know that my procedures were sound and my ideas were useful and creative. Still, I felt like I lacked something—class, education, finesse, normalness—something I couldn't quite identify. It seemed to me, despite what I now see as a mountain of evidence, that others got something from somebody somewhere along the way that I didn't get. And there were those times when I said something stupid, or didn't know some fact that was common knowledge, or felt disgust for myself or a loved one, that confirmed an innate flaw.

I would not discuss said flaw with anybody until I was in my early thirties and dating a psychiatrist named Neil. And, no, I didn't discuss it with him; I discussed it with *his* therapist! Every time I would mention a new book or an audiotape to Neil, he would smile this knowing smile—the guy must have been a wonderful therapist—and say, "I know, but it's not the way I do it; I do it with Greg." Greg was his therapist. After months of this, I thought I must be missing something . . . or maybe I just had permission from this charming, handsome psychiatrist to do what I had always wanted to do. I scheduled therapy. Neil seemed happy for me, but also apprehensive. He knew how important it was to use a "good" therapist. Reluctantly, he suggested I call his *personal* therapist. I am still grateful.

Therapy, I thought, was as wonderful as food—everybody should have it. Sitting in that office and saying things out loud for the first time and crying on the way home changed my life. It seemed all I had to do to change something was confess it, and voilà! If I admitted to feeling self-conscious, the next day in the elevator I was smiling and making somebody else feel more comfortable. I had landed in paradise . . . okay, really I had just made it over another hurdle, albeit a significant one. I would continue to raise the bar, because meeting it still left me wanting.

I remember an earlier romance: the man I was dating, the man I thought I loved, asked me to marry him. I thought, "Why in the world didn't you ask me before I built this house—I don't even have blinds up yet!" I was so set on reaching the next bar, on making the picture perfect, that I didn't really know what I felt. He was a self-made millionaire; I was a midtwenties, sheltered divorcee. I didn't want nice things because he could give them to me. I wanted nice things because I deserved them . . . and I had to prove to myself that I did. I thought if I earned the money to pay for them that that would mean I deserved them. And I was beginning to think that I wanted to start my own business to make some *real* money before being handed a partnership. I remember wondering what else I would have to do and where it would end. When would I give myself permission to just be happy? Therapy helped me get one big step closer, but I wasn't there yet.

Many of the young women I meet take another path: they are intent on being married and having a baby. When a man proposes marriage, they say yes to marriage without fully considering the man they are saying yes to. I know this—I have said yes to more engagements than I have marriages. Instead of looking for what we want in a man, we say yes to a man who *thinks* he sees what he wants in us. Aah, it feels good to be wanted, and when we're afraid it might not happen again, we say yes. It's as though we're saying yes to being wanted and living happily ever after—not yes to a particular man. But it's the man we get!

Neither scenario—saying yes to a "savior" or trying harder to attract a more viable savior—leaves room for knowing and loving who we are *without* the trappings. We are caught trying to make the picture perfect, without making sure that it reflects who we are. We are like an interior designer who sets out to create an exquisite home without first getting to know those who will live there, or a matchmaker who sets out to find a partner for somebody without first getting to know them, for fear that knowing them would mess up the plan.

I counseled a young woman who was heartbroken because her fiancé had called off the wedding. She sobbed in disbelief, "How could he not want to marry me?" She had prepared the bride—painstakingly molded her body at the gym, groomed herself to perfection, still maintained her job as a physician's assistant and the house she had paid for herself. She didn't know who she *really* was, but she thought she was the perfect "wife-to-be." She kept rehearsing what she could have done better: Maybe she should have initiated sex instead of waiting for him. She could have been more outgoing with his friends. Maybe she catered to him too much. She was not yet ready to find herself. She was still struggling to meet somebody else's criteria for "good enough."

Like the young woman, often we have worked so hard to create the perfect picture that we don't want to give up on it. We don't want to waste it. We don't want to accept that we—and everybody else—are *innately* good. We want our hard work to make us special (read: better than everybody else). It can't. But it's not wasted. Whatever it takes to get us to the truth is worth the effort. Until we believe there is something more, though, we want to hold on to what we can see. And if it's not enough to satisfy, we raise the bar, move the finish line, set a new standard. And we try harder.

I showed my employees and coworkers a spare-me-the-excuses attitude. I wanted to get the job done—fast. I was smart enough to realize that by itself the job wasn't enough to make me feel good about my life or myself, and I inevitably had a business to go home to that I felt more passionate about, the one that was going to set me up financially. And I kept writing vignettes that

I wanted to compile for a book. And I added teaching the illiterate—even got certified—to feeding the hungry and employing the jobless. Those were the people I could relate to. I hadn't given up on the dream; I couldn't bring myself to settle for the day job. I would entertain the dream, but I couldn't seem to find enough time to do it justice. I would also entertain a series of men, one at a time, long enough for them to fall in love with me, and long enough for me to wonder if I could do better. And because I hoped doing better would make me feel good enough, I kept trying. It was only later that I realized how much my relationships served to feed my ego—but the ego is a bottomless pit; it is not the same as self-esteem.

The Ego Is Not the True Self

The ego is conjured up by fear. Every major religion, despite the differences in terminology, would help you to be rid of it to reach your true self. Your true self is the divine within that transcends the physical—whether you prefer to think of it as Spirit, God, Allah, Tao, or Brahman. During the Tang Dynasty, it is said that the Chinese prime minister visited the temple. And although he considered himself a devout and humble Buddhist, he asked the master to explain the Buddha's perspective on egotism. The master answered in a condescending tone, "What kind of stupid question is that?" The prime minister was outraged. "How dare you speak to me in that manner!" he shouted back. The master's expression softened. "That, Your Excellency, is egotism."

Rooted in fear, the ego is ugly. And people see it even when we don't realize we're exposing it. Still we cling to it—bury our true selves with it—because without it, we would have to face our pain. Whether we realize it or not, we have customized the ego to shield our wounds or those spots we see as vulnerable.

One of my clients, Steve, a male nurse, came to me wanting to know why women dumped him. He was, after all, a professional, good-looking, very caring man. He had gone to great lengths to take care of himself (the gym five days a week) and his home (tasteful art, flower-lined walks). But he wasn't a doctor. Of course, that doesn't really matter—unless he thinks it does. Steve is in what's still a mostly female profession, and he's "constantly reminded by friends" that he's a nurse. Even his son came home from school one day and said, "Dad, you're a doctor, right?" Steve said, "No, son, I'm a nurse—you know that." His son said, "No, you must be a doctor; Ritchie said men can't be nurses." He had worked hard. He did his job well. He led a "balanced" life. But he didn't feel good enough to go to medical school, and all these years later, he still didn't feel good enough. He lacked self-esteem, and because his ego was let down by his job, he *also* lacked the feigned confidence demonstrated by many men even when they do lack self-esteem. So, while he attracted women with his physique, he failed to keep their attention. He was left wanting but wasn't sure why—or even exactly what he wanted. But he was, once again, heartbroken.

I have watched another man as he pressed on. Creating a successful business wasn't enough. He would get bored, wanting more than money and business success. He would buy another car, then a faster car, then a plane. He would take up ballroom dancing and then Spanish—both the language and dancing. But somewhere in there, his wife would leave him. And finally, devastated, he would begin to look within—but he was still hanging on to his empire. I could feel his fear as he clung steadfastly to what he knew, to what he had learned so well to control, to what he had worked for that made him "superior" to others.

When we serve ego, we are bound to be left wanting—rung after rung after rung of the proverbial ladder. Perhaps you blame your parents, your spouse, or the government. Maybe you hate your employer. Maybe you have developed a blatant inferiority or superiority complex. Maybe you clench everything you can get your hands on for fear that the rug will be yanked out from under you. Maybe you flaunt your money—always picking up the check, sending gifts or limos. Whatever you do, you do because you hurt. You don't know how to ease the pain, so you disguise it. You may not even feel the pain long enough to know it's there—your knee-jerk reaction is to defend yourself and control what you can.

Defensive and controlling behavior is unloving, though, so you feel worse instead of better. Being a "witch" or a "jerk" is your worst nightmare; it only reinforces the notion that you fall short, or that you're somehow "different." It also drives you to try harder (or give up). You can't quite get enough, though. First you want more, then you need more—whether it is money, food, drugs, sex, accomplishment, education, looks, or religious insurance. It's easy to get stuck on a treadmill parked at self-esteem in Maslow's hierarchy of needs.

According to the late psychologist Abraham Maslow's theory of human motivation, we are motivated to meet our most basic survival needs before moving on to more meaningful ones. Until our basic needs for air, water, food, and sleep are met, our primary motivation is to meet them. Then we can move on to growth needs of love and belonging, esteem, and self-esteem. And then we can move up to meet our self-actualization or fulfillment needs.

If Maslow was right, until we have met our physiological needs, we are preoccupied by those. We could argue here that dealing with rejection—the signal that something is wrong with us and needs to be corrected—is a survival need. Regardless, until we have dealt with both our bodies and our egos, we are stuck worrying about what other people think of us. Until we have *shed* our egos to find our essence, we cannot satisfy our need for self-esteem. *Self*-esteem, or self-verification, can only be had by aligning our behavior with our true self.

The problem is that we don't know who we are, and until we give up the false notion imposed on us of who we are, we are unlikely to look inward. So we stay on the treadmill. Mind you, we might even be trying to align with goodness, but it's tough to find goodness while we're shielding our divinity with our egos. And as long as our goodness is contingent on something outside ourselves, we will not feel good enough. We will feel as though we're trying to be something we're not.

Not feeling good enough after we've spent ourselves trying to be can be very scary. We inevitably open the door to the evils of fear—anxiety, shame, envy, anger, blame, hatred, pride, and guilt—which reinforces the notion that we fall short and drives us to try harder or give up. Trying so hard just to come up wanting is discouraging. And whether we plow forward for more "success" or give up and try to drown our grief, we can only temporarily escape our feelings.

CHAPTER THREE

Perpetuating the Striving and the Lack

> As long as anyone believes that
> his ideal and purpose is outside him,
> that it is above the clouds, in the past or
> in the future, he will go outside himself
> and seek fulfillment where it cannot be found.
> He will look for solutions and answers
> at every point except where they
> can be found—in himself.
>
> —Erich Fromm

OUR FEELINGS OF inferiority are not date stamped; they are simply filed away in our unconscious, where there is no sense of time. And no matter how old or "successful" we are, we can find data to reinforce our feelings and thus perpetuate our struggle to meet some prerequisite for being good enough. Even when we've met one prerequisite or sixty prerequisites, we come up with another one. Why? Because meeting the first sixty leaves us wanting. If we still feel inadequate, we must still be inadequate, right? Wrong. But there will always be something we can do better or something else we can do. That something might be worthwhile; it might even be a valid part of our truth, our values, our essence, and love. But doing it—unless we see it as a manifestation of our innate goodness—does not make us feel good enough. We can spend our lives in service befitting a saint and still *feel* inadequate.

Mother Teresa herself revealed the emptiness she felt in years of letters to her spiritual directors published in *Mother Teresa: Come Be My Light.* Following is one such letter:

> Now Father—since 49 or 50 this terrible sense of loss—this untold darkness—this loneliness this continual longing for God—which gives me that pain deep down in my heart—Darkness is such that I really do not see—neither with my mind nor with my reason—the place of God in my soul is blank—There is no God in me—when the pain of longing is so great—I just long & long for God—and then it is that I feel—He does not want me—He is not there—. . . God does not want me—Sometimes—I just hear my own heart cry out—"My God" and nothing else comes—The torture and pain I can't explain—

Mother Teresa, despite a life committed to the poorest of the poor, despite the admiration of millions for her compassion and service, felt our pain. "If I ever become a Saint," she said, "I will surely be one of 'darkness.' I will continually be absent from

Heaven—to light the light of those in darkness on earth." I can't comprehend exactly where Mother Teresa is, but I think she has found peace . . . and that she is fulfilling her "prophecy." And I am with all of my heart, in the best way I know how, saying thank you.

Reward

Short of finding our own light within, we are rewarded for "good" behavior—and we grow attached to the rewards. After all, for those of us who are not saints, they meet real needs for acceptance and approval. It starts with something like a cookie and grows into a trip to the park and then a new bike. Later, it's a new dress, a promotion, sex, a trip, maybe even a new house, a new boyfriend, or a plaque honoring our virtue. And as long as we think our "good" behavior is being rewarded, we're motivated to keep up the good work! The rewards, however, are about as good as the behavior. That's not to say that the behavior or the rewards are bad, only that they are what they are. What if we were taught to feel what it feels like inside when we share a toy? What if we were taught to recognize the pain behind somebody's anger and help him move beyond it; and what if we were taught to revel in how good it feels to make a difference for somebody? And what if all we had to do to be a great teacher was to overcome our fear? What if we didn't have to have a Ph.D., a successful business, or a house on the ocean to help people? And, what if we were taught that the feeling of *being* good *was* the reward (no cookies necessary)?

Let's be clear, though; as long as we are receiving rewards, it's difficult to walk away from them. And as long as we're clinging to rewards for doing what society finds acceptable, we are clinging to a facade. We are reinforcing a facade, which offers us a false sense of security. And as long as we cling to the facade, we will not find the goodness that lies buried beneath it. Ironically, the rewards of being true to our essence far exceed the rewards of even the loftiest of facades.

Punishment

When we fall short, we reinforce the notion that we *generally* fall short. A mistake becomes "I can't do anything right." Again, we see how we are programmed to notice the negative. Thus, we validate our worst fear. And when "bad" things happen, as they inevitably will, we may take them on as our punishment—or our destiny. For years my marriage and divorce haunted me. One of them must have been a mistake. Which one? And did it matter? I could take neither of them back. If the marriage was the mistake, was I suppose to live with it until death? If the divorce was a mistake, was I suppose to remarry my ex-husband? He didn't want to remarry me, and I don't know what I would have done if he had. Maybe the marriage and divorce were both mistakes, and I was a bumbling idiot. Was I to make amends? Could I? Was I destined to be alone for the rest of my life as punishment?

Even after we escape the watchful eye and the swift punishment of a parent, we find ourselves watching out for God's judgment—and everybody else's. But I no longer believe that God punishes us. I believe he simply lets us pay the consequences of our actions, not to punish us, but to allow us to learn. Understandably, given the hardness of our heads, it sometimes looks as though we're getting hit with the proverbial frying pan. I remember a minister named Clarence saying that God loved his little girl Cheryl (who was a grown woman at the time) more than he did. Clarence was a softy. He had a hard time watching anybody—especially his only little girl—struggle. He and God had been friends for a long time, though, and he knew God loved us enough to let us find our own way, even when it was painful, even if we kept triggering the "frying pan."

You've probably looked on as a parent's patience was slowly (or quickly) eroded as their child kept asking for—or demanding, as the case may be—a candy bar or another toy or a carnival ride after eating three hot dogs. It's easier to give in. But God does not take the easy way out at our expense. He lets us get the lesson, and, yes, sometimes that means we get another toy, but he lets us pay for it with our own money. We cannot escape consequences, what Buddhists and Hindus call karma and Sir Isaac Newton called Law III (for every action there is a reaction).

The God I believe in doesn't punish us. He lets us learn at our own pace. If we fail first grade, he's not the sort of proud parent who pushes us forward anyway. He just keeps believing in us. Even if we fail first grade three times, he doesn't push us through the system. He lets us keep trying until we get it. *He* knows what we're made of! Like a good therapist, though, he knows we have to find out for ourselves.

Rejection

We worry about more than just rejection. We worry about getting overlooked, being taken advantage of, losing ground, and getting replaced as this week's favorite. When something happens to threaten our ego, our response seems disproportionate—so what if we go bald? We don't perceive it as our hair falling out; we perceive it as our ego tumbling down to reveal the truth that we're inferior, which is not really the truth, but our worst fear. Even when we really do get turned down (by a lover, an employer, or a bank), it simply means that we didn't meet the criteria set out at the time by a particular person or entity for a particular slot, or that somebody else who was also available fit the slot better than we did. Yet we often read that "rejection" as a confirmation, whether we admit or not, that we don't quite measure up, that we don't fit in, and that we just might be doomed. How else can we explain the pain of rejection—particularly in a romantic context?

When somebody sits on my sofa and wraps her arms around her abdomen as if to contain the pain, it's about more than the loss of a four-month-old relationship. When somebody picks up the phone and calls me at 9:00 PM, afraid of interrupting my evening but more afraid of the pain, it's about more than the woman he met last month. When we think we have found the love of our life and lose it, we lose more than that person. At least it can feel as though we do. We lose the fairy tale. We lose everything we hoped and dreamed of in a relationship, all the joy and fulfillment, all the love. We also lose what we thought was finally going to make everything else okay, what was somehow going to complete us and make us okay. Even when we know the relationship fell short of what we wanted, we might think it was our best shot at it—or our *only* shot at it. We might think we got lucky. We might think we are never going to get that lucky again.

When we personalize rejection, we personalize somebody else's preferences or standards. We beat ourselves up—often without looking to see if we buy into their preferences. Somebody might give you the cold shoulder because he prefers blonds. Come on! If you really wanted to be blond, you could be. There's no reason for that to hurt. A prospective employer may cut you before the first interview because you are overqualified. There is no reason for that to hurt—unless you and your insecurity leap to the conclusion that you are not good enough.

You might be thinking that you're more apt to get angry—or "get even"—than hurt. There is no anger without pain, though! We might be in such a big hurry to be rid of the pain that we feel it only for a split second, without even being aware of it. But pain always lurks behind anger or any negative emotion. You can deny the pain or cover it with anger or defensiveness, but you can only heal it with love.

Whether you feel pain or anger, you probably rationalize it and, perhaps, blame somebody else for it. Defensiveness and justification are red flags that can lead us to the truth, and the truth is always a friend (even when it's painful). We can't heal what's causing the pain unless we're willing to face it. If we simply justify our feelings and label our subsequent behavior as self-defense, we might be off the hook temporarily, but we won't learn from our feelings or assume responsibility for our actions. And what's hurting behind the negative emotion continues to hurt.

Another means of dealing with the pain is to beat yourself up. You may rehearse what happened over and over in your mind, evaluating what you could have done or what you should have done. If you tend to be perfectionistic, it can be difficult for you to accept a "mistake," though. And until you do, you are unlikely to learn something from it. You are unlikely to move on. You might stay in a miserable rut instead.

Sometimes our emotions run the gamut. An unemployed fifty-two-year-old woman continued to e-mail me for months after seeking my advice. Initially she agreed that she had to assume responsibility for her predicament and take steps to create the life she wanted. In the face of rejection during the next few months, though, she would blame her family for not helping her, label prospective employers cruel for asking about gaps in her employment, and badmouth the United States government for not providing her with a job when she had an engineering degree. She would also whine about "overpaying" for the lousy work somebody—who was supposed to be a professional—did on her résumé. She would bemoan having sent the résumé out before correcting the professional's mistakes and belabor the pros and cons of both applying in person and applying by mail. She would also complain of near-fainting episodes and a possible nervous disorder and refuse to speak to her aunt who suggested she might be depressed. And she would contemplate moving to Alaska or Sweden. And she would run through segments of this routine over and over—as though she didn't remember that she had been through them before. She was on a treadmill but seemed oblivious to the repetition of the belt.

We don't simply get stuck, though. We develop bad habits; we get addicted. Addiction is a means of trying to escape the pain and fill a need with something that can never really fill it. Our negative emotion fuels the desire to escape, thus resulting in addiction, depression, chronic pain, and disease. The consequences are flagrant: materialism, obesity, an overtaxed healthcare system, burgeoning social services, overrated sex, workaholism, knowledge without wisdom, obsession, and fear-based religion.

Our unemployed friend had been without a job before. She was overweight and thought she might be addicted to shopping. And while her family may have wanted to help, they seemed at wits' end. She would eventually accuse her father of joining her brother, the attorney, in a conspiracy against her. She never really felt as though being an engineer was "good enough," but she was petrified of trying to follow her brother's footsteps into law school. Had her father put aside his insecurity to really see his daughter (and himself), he might have offered his blessing on another path, one that his daughter could pursue with confidence and passion. He was likely doing the best he could, and maybe he even thought he was helping his daughter by pushing her toward law.

When we give children the message that their goodness or our acceptance is based on their meeting certain criteria, we set the stage for them to be unhappy—whether they meet the criteria or not. They never feel truly "good." They feel pressured and, often, misplaced. They are likely to plod on, like their parents, not knowing who they are. And they cannot recognize their worth until they do.

Parents pass on their insecurities, ironically, because they feel compelled to provide their children with more than they had. And that's a surefire way to perpetuate the striving and the lack. The best gift we can give a child is an awareness of his innate goodness.

Part Two

Dead Ends
and What They
Teach Us

[MAN] HAS TO DISCOVER THAT
ACCUMULATION IS NOT REALIZATION.
IT IS THE INNER LIGHT THAT REVEALS
HIM, NOT OUTER THINGS.

—RABINDRANATH TAGORE

MUST WE DO something to *make* ourselves good enough? Can we? Must we follow the dead ends in our pursuit? Must we spin our wheels at self-esteem, and for how long before we realize that our goodness has been with us all along?

Often it is only in reaching the absolute finality of a dead end that we are at last willing to consciously look at the lie that we are not good enough. When we have exhausted our hope of salvation in the next rung of the ladder and the escape, we let go of them and find the truth—we are innately good—which is the key we want to pass on to our children. It is no coincidence that individual studies point to self-esteem as our number one need and to meaning (found in self-actualization at the top of Maslow's hierarchy of needs) as our number one goal. We look for self-esteem in the wrong places. We look for it where we find esteem from others (based on what they can readily quantify). It is not there. And we postpone meaning until we have found it. That's how we get stuck with neither.

Food, sex, accomplishment, knowledge, beauty, and spirituality are intended for our satisfaction and fulfillment. They are a confirmation that we are living our truth—that is what makes them truly gratifying. When I got a contract for this book, it was not the prospect of money or acclaim that stirred my heart but rather the affirmation of my belief. I believe that when we align with love and follow where it leads us, that good will come from it and we'll be afforded the privilege of sharing that good.

We don't give up the things that are intended for our satisfaction and fulfillment. We revel in them. But we are no longer motivated by ego to pursue them. We are no longer obsessed, afraid to stop and face the pain and ourselves. We no longer postpone what we truly want, as though we instinctively know we are not yet ready for it. Love naturally balances our lives with all good things, because love is everything good. And as we love ourselves, we nurture body, mind, and spirit.

As we move through the dead ends and what they teach us in the chapters to come, consider the following warning signs of a destructive habit or an addiction and keep in mind that you probably have more than one to free yourself from:

- Denial, with a sense that your security is threatened

- Chronic destructive behavior and escalation because of higher tolerance

- Mood-altered state

- Inability to stop in the face of negative consequences

- Withdrawal symptoms

Chances are you started out with honorable intentions—like I did. Smile. Sigh. Smile. Of course we want to look good, make enough money, and be our best. We get sucked in because we can't seem to look quite good enough, or earn enough money, or accomplish enough to make us feel the way we want to feel—

good enough. Instead of realizing that immediately, we go for more . . . and we keep moving the finish line, all the while thinking—if we are still thinking—that the next goal or the next rung on the proverbial ladder is "the one."

That said, if self-gratification didn't feel good (albeit not good enough), it would be easier to exchange it for living our truth. Self-gratification inevitably gets old, though, and when it does, our truth is still there. The examined life depicts both the joy and the sorrow of self-gratification and makes a case for finding greater joy and sweeter sorrow.

CHAPTER FOUR

Money/"Stuff"

NOT WHAT WE HAVE BUT WHAT WE ENJOY
CONSTITUTES OUR ABUNDANCE.

—EPICURUS

MONEY, AS THEY say, is a lousy means of keeping score.

The baby boomers are not the first to demonstrate how to fill a life with everything money can buy, but perhaps they have best demonstrated how to have a winning score and still lose. Ouch. In 1922 when American families gathered around a radio to hear the first daily program, only 60,000 homes *had* a radio. Today, the average home has a whopping eight radios—eliminating any need for the family to meet in one room—and the radios play second (or fifth, as the case may be) to televisions, computers, CD players, and iPods. And, according to the U.S. Census Bureau, disposable incomes and personal spending more than doubled between 1969 and 1996. Most people (the people we know from "average homes") don't need more money; they *want* more money. And they don't want it for what it will buy; they want it because they think what it will buy (more radios and less time together!?) will bring them happiness. It won't.

It seems we have to learn that lesson for ourselves, though, and most of us are still collecting evidence (read: dollars and "stuff"). The more time we spend in the sole pursuit of money, the more empty our lives become. Emptiness underscores all of our doubts about who we are and fuels the fear that we may never be happy or good enough. Fear is the mother of all negative emotion, including anger, resentment, anxiousness, and defensiveness. The more we act out, the more we clash with others, and the more we confirm that we are misfits. Either that, or everybody else is an "asshole"—and we don't *really* believe they're to blame!

But the deeper our void, the more hopeless we feel, and the more we need a means of proving that we're okay. If we can't prove it to ourselves, maybe we can at least prove it to others. We continue to pursue what we eventually know is nothing more than a dead end in terms of happiness. When we have some financial security—and that's all we have—we don't want to let go of it. We continue, then, with what brings us esteem from others, and a sense of control, over something. We'd rather be rich and eccentric than poor and crazy.

We refuse to be unhappy and unsuccessful. And we haven't *totally* given up on happy—we know fleeting moments of happy, and part of us thinks that just maybe if we could double our annual income, or our net worth, or earn as much as our mentor, we'd feel like it was enough. Then we could step back and enjoy life.

Money remains the most widely used quantifier of success, making it difficult to feel successful without it . . . until you have accumulated enough to realize that there is not enough money to buy self-esteem or, as the Beatles' song says, love. Money seems to be the cure-all, until you're sick—physically, mentally, emotionally, or spiritually. Then the true value of money is revealed. It buys things, nice things—but however nice, they are things.

Christmas after Christmas, I have cried while watching *It's a Wonderful Life*. George Bailey, played by Jimmy Stewart, is finally exasperated with being the good guy when his absentminded uncle misplaces $8,000 of the Bailey Building and Loan's money. George doesn't have $8,000 to put back in the kitty, and he can't face the bank examiner that afternoon and the subsequent scandal and prison term. He is worth more dead than alive because of a life insurance policy. And as he contemplates jumping off the snow-covered bridge across town, Clarence, his guardian angel, jumps into the icy cold water and screams for help, knowing George will jump in to save him. He does!

When Clarence introduces himself to George as his guardian angel, George says (in disbelief, but kindly), "Well, you look about like the kind of angel I'd get." Perhaps mustering a bit of hope, though, George asks, "You don't happen to have eight thousand bucks on you, do you?"

"No, we don't use money in heaven," Clarence giggles.

"Comes in pretty handy down here, bub," George says.

George drives an old car and lives in an old house. After his father dies, he puts his kid brother, Harry, through college and keeps the Bailey Building and Loan office running in the hometown he has been trying to leave for years. He watches, mostly undaunted, as his brother goes into research with his new in-laws, and his friend Sam Wainwright goes to the big city and makes a fortune in plastics. He turns down an offer from Mr. Potter, the bitter old man who owns most of the town and wants George and his Bailey Building and Loan, too. He realizes that the trips to Europe and furs for his wife that Potter tries to tempt him with aren't worth his soul. But now he is at the end of his rope. Even his guardian angel can't conjure up the money he needs.

Clarence is about to earn his wings, though. He shows George what life in his hometown would have come to without him, and what his wife would have come to without him. Turns out she would have turned down the plastics mogul and lived out her life as a librarian. George gets a second wind as he gets a good look at who he really is and what his life has meant. His is "a wonderful life," indeed.

At the end of the movie, George is shown with his wife— ever at his side—and kids standing behind a table receiving a parade of folks and money. His brother flies in, leaving the office of the president of the United States, just shy of formally receiving the Congressional Medal of Honor. And the plastics mogul Sam Wainwright wires from London that his office is prepared to advance George "up to $25,000. Heehaw and Merry Christmas!"

When we realize our innate goodness, we want to align with it. And we are well on our way to self-verification. Then, nothing else matters! But everything else is there!

Today we have people with more money than they know what to do with who are still looking for an escape route, because they can't find their goodness. They jump off proverbial bridges (and sometimes real ones) and check into rehab, without a guardian angel who can show them how much difference their life has meant. Elvis Presley, who was in so many ways "the King," died at forty-two with an overdose of prescription drugs in his system. A recent headline read "The Queen of Mean Leaves $US12m to Dog." You decide if the words published by AFP (a global news agency) describe a happy person:

Leona Helmsley, the late US hotel billionaire known as the "Queen of Mean," has lived up to her reputation even in death, cutting two grandchildren out of her will and leaving US$12 million to her dog.

Trouble, a white Maltese, received the largest bequest from Helmsley's will, which was read out in a New York court on Tuesday.

The will sets aside a trust to care for the pampered pooch, which once starred in advertisements for Helmsley's hotel chain, and also stipulates that the dog be buried beside her and her late husband, Harry, who died in 1997.

The family's luxury mausoleum is to be maintained in perpetuity thanks to a further US$3 million trust.

Helmsley, famed for observing that "only the little people pay taxes" and who spent time in jail for tax fraud, died earlier this month aged 87.

She earned herself the sobriquet "the Queen of Mean" for her hard-nosed work ethic, short temper and reputation for cruelty and penny-pinching.

Helmsley was survived by her brother—who received US$10 million and will look after Trouble until the pooch dies—as well as four grandchildren and 12 great-grandchildren. The two grand-sons who were included in the will received US$5 million each, but only on the proviso that they visit their late father's grave at least once a year.

Her two other grandchildren were cut out "for reasons which are known to them," according to the will.

The lion's share of her $US4 billion dollar fortune goes to unnamed causes through a charitable trust.

Freud theorized that as long as things were going well, a man let his ego do all sorts of things, but when misfortune befell him, he heightened the demands of his conscience. Perhaps that helps to explain why Jesus said that it was easier for a camel to go through the eye of a needle than for a rich man to enter the king-dom of heaven. Still, we seek money as though it can buy happi-ness, the same happiness we forgo in the chase.

How much do we have to accumulate before we recognize it for what it is—a lousy means of keeping score—when there need be no score at all?

CHAPTER FIVE

Appearance

AND BEAUTY IS NOT A NEED BUT AN ECSTASY.
IT IS NOT A MOUTH THIRSTING NOR AN EMPTY HAND
STRETCHED FORTH, BUT RATHER A HEART ENFLAMED
AND A SOUL ENCHANTED. BEAUTY IS ETERNITY
GAZING AT ITSELF IN A MIRROR. BUT YOU ARE
ETERNITY AND YOU ARE THE MIRROR.

—KAHLIL GIBRAN

THE MEDIA HOSTS an ongoing parade of beautiful people. They even offer commentary on the most beautiful eyes, lips, and buttocks, helping us to embrace both a false sense of normal and a false sense of ideal. There is no ideal. And there certainly is no ideal for everybody—5'10" cannot be ideal for a woman who is 5'4". I know this! Yet studies show that the vast majority of women are uncomfortable with their looks, particularly their bodies. They want to look more like the picture in the maga-zine—often the one they cannot possibly look like.

And a growing number of men—because they live to be older, stay active longer, and marry women half their age (I'm funny, not bitter, really)—are now fueling the accelerated growth of an industry developed to make us look good enough. More liberated women are giving men a taste of how it feels to be gawked at, reveled in, *and* critiqued. Some of them are well prepared for it; some are scurrying; some are bewildered.

Women, though, are more apt to be trapped in their innate desire to please men. The author of the creation story, whoever he—or, perhaps, she—was, nailed this correctly. And measuring up to the ideal that they *think* men want weighs on them, the same as being strong or powerful weighs on many men. Think about it, though . . . the average man is *under* 5'10". The average woman, by the way, is about 5'4"! Not a bad match for the aver-age man—but there is no ideal match (anymore than there is an ideal height or an ideal hair color or an ideal set of features)! I think God made my husband 6'3" just to remove any remnant of doubt I harbored (he jokingly tells me I'm every bit of 5'10", a height he could well accommodate)!

Sometimes the media include somebody like "Ugly Betty," but notice how they make it clear that they are presenting ugly, or dorky, or clumsy! You may think you're above it. Most people aren't. Keep in mind that you begin to get the message as a child, and the message hits hard with adolescence when appearance takes on vastly increased importance. We get the message . . . and we know everybody else gets the same one. It is difficult to be above the message *and* everybody else. So we must try, we must do our best, to meet some misguided standard—only to fall mostly, yes, short.

We can, even from a shallow perspective, find some reassurance in studies that indicate that people actually find "average" features to be the most attractive (Langlois and Roggman 1990; Rhodes et al. 1999). If you're not average, perhaps you're one of those people with striking features. You are striking, if you think you are. In the movie *The Mirror Has Two Faces,* the character played by Barbra Streisand grew up thinking she was unattractive. She was a gifted professor, very funny—but pretty, she was not. Her sister—the pretty one—decided to respond to a personal ad for Barbra, making sure to include a photo so that the man was not expecting someone attractive. The man, as luck would have it, was a very attractive, albeit boring, math professor from across campus who was easily sucked into physical relationships that didn't work. He was looking for delightful, intelligent, funny, but definitely *not* hot. And, thus, an enchanting, but nonphysical marriage relationship developed between Barbra and the math professor, played by Jeff Bridges. But, alas, Barbra faced the pain she felt as the ugly duckling, only to realize that the proverbial mirror had two faces looking back at her, and one of them was very beautiful. Like our goodness, the beautiful is always there. We don't *really* see it on the outside, though, until we see it on the inside. When you see it, others will see it. *Nothing* says you're attractive like you do.

And there are some undeniable advantages to being attractive. Attractive people are generally perceived as more poised, interesting, sociable, independent, exciting, sexual, intelligent, well adjusted, and successful (as well as more vain and materialistic)! And in study after study, physical attractiveness has overwhelmed everything else as the best predictor of how well a person would be liked after a first meeting. And first impressions, as we know, are challenging to overcome. No wonder people get stuck trying to *make* themselves more attractive.

But let's look at the correlation between a first impression and a self-impression. A first impression is based on hygiene, dress, and body language. We care for ourselves, dress ourselves, and move our bodies based on how we see ourselves. When Barbra started to see herself as beautiful, she presented herself differently—she was exercising and getting her hair done as though she were pretty! And Jeff Bridges, by the way, was wowed. Not surprising, especially given a study (Lewandowski 2007) showing that men and women who exhibit positive traits, such as honesty and helpfulness, are perceived as better looking. Those who exhibit negative traits, such as unfairness and rudeness, appear to be less physically attractive to observers.

Sure, we can fool some of the people, but most are skilled at discerning how genuine you are—even when they aren't skilled at picking up on other qualities. It's interesting to note here that not everybody cares how sincere you are. Many people want to know what you offer *them*. Maybe you're a valuable friend or contact, or somebody "beneath" them to keep at arm's length. In other words, they're trying to meet their own needs—or nurse their own insecurity.

We're all looking for "enoughness" . . . many of us in the area of attractiveness. Because we can't really find it in attractiveness, we struggle. We diet, we shop for more and better clothes, trying to find the ones that make us look good enough. We lose weight, buy tinted contacts, try different makeup, have laser peels and surgeries. We resort to gold watches and big diamonds, and even "trophy" spouses (yes, women, as well as men, can go for a trophy).

How big is big enough? How smooth is smooth enough? How expensive is expensive enough? How thin is thin enough to make you feel good enough? Anorexia is a poignant example of how getting "thin enough" does not provide us with what we're seeking. There is no getting thin enough when what we're really trying to do is get good enough.

Without self-esteem, no amount of money, technology, or reinforcement from other people will be enough. Here's an example from my e-mail:

Dear Jan:

I am looking for some insight. I met a really attractive and intelligent woman at a public event in a museum. We talked for thirty minutes and really seemed to hit it off. Then things suddenly went downhill. I commented that she had a "nice hourglass figure." I thought she would take it as a compliment. Instead, she became deeply offended. She snapped, "Oh really . . . well perhaps I should do some plus-size modeling!" and then she slapped my face and walked off in a huff. I will never forget the immediate aftermath—the sound of her high heels hitting the hardwood floor, the murmur of the crowd, and the stares, as I'm standing there alone rubbing my cheek.

She had the classic figure of a 1950s' pinup—large bust, narrow waist, shapely hips/legs. I guess she interpreted "hourglass" as meaning big/overweight/full-figured. I thought it meant shapely and well proportioned. When I told a friend, she shook her head and said it was never a good idea to comment on a woman's figure, even if I thought it was complimentary. . . .

Saying "you have nice long legs" to a woman who thinks she has sexy legs is interpreted as a compliment. But it might trigger pain in a woman with the same figure if she was teased about her lanky legs and is still self-conscious about them. And pain can be quickly masked by anger. When a woman has learned to love herself—all of herself—a man can pay her a sincere compliment without *anybody* getting a slap in the face.

Until then, even a compliment that's received with a smile can lead to disappointment. We can feel good for the moment and get our hopes up—only to feel the same way when we look in the mirror again. It's analogous to buying a new hat, or a new dress, or a new car. It feels good at first—and it can even get us through a temporary setback. But it can't change our opinion of our worth. Oh, we might decide that we're better looking, or realize that more women are attracted to a new sports car, or that sales clerks pay more attention to well-dressed shoppers. Those observations don't translate to self-esteem, though!

With self-esteem, money and technology can only hope to make us *look* as good as we feel. And there's no harm in using what's available to us to take care of our bodies. When we love who we are, we demonstrate that, but we are not motivated by fear. We are motivated by love. We don't take care of ourselves to feel good enough; we take care of ourselves because we *know* how worthwhile we are.

As Jimmy Buffet might say, our bodies are temples—not tents.

CHAPTER SIX

Religion

GOD HAS NO RELIGION.

—MAHATMA GANDHI

I GREW UP with religion. And I had no idea it wasn't God's. The little girl trying to do the right thing would grow into a young woman with a list of dos and don'ts used as an insurance policy. It would take me years to realize that I didn't just carry the list as a ticket into heaven—I didn't really know if it would get me in—I carried it as a measuring stick to measure my goodness against everybody else's. It was my self-righteous cloak. I would go to church three times a week. I would abstain from drinking, dancing, movies, and any makeup that couldn't pass as natural. We were instructed, after all, to avoid the very appearance of evil and not to indulge in something that might make someone else stumble. You see, even if I thought it was okay to dance, if somebody else thought it was a sin, to him it would be a sin. So I better not dance, lest I cause him to sin. I had a double dose of worrying about what everybody thought of me—my mother and religion!

Going to church three times a week didn't make me feel good enough, though. It reminded me that I was not. And it reminded me that I was just a stumble away from going to hell. I was divorced (after much deliberation) and twenty-five before I sat down with that refreshingly intellectual Presbyterian minister and—quietly, in the privacy of my own living room—asked irreverent questions. I was trying to look objectively at what I believed versus what I had been taught. He did not take the Bible literally, and he did not interpret it the way my church did. He had never believed what I felt guilty for questioning.

My questions screamed out my naïveté and fear of mocking the doctrine that distracted me from love. I wanted to know if it was a sin to dance with somebody besides your husband. I wanted to know if it was really a sin to have oral sex *with* your husband. I wanted to know how the four Gospels could contradict each other, and if it was okay to tithe my income *after* taxes. The other questions escape me. Mostly what I remember is that a huge weight was lifted. I no longer had to believe what I was unable to believe, nor did I have to carry around the guilt of betrayal. But decades later, I realize how many questions I was still afraid to ask.

As a young woman, I had a classic case of cognitive dissonance—there was too much disparity between my thinking (when I was able to separate it from my indoctrination) and my behavior. I grew up learning to behave a certain way. And because changing my behavior was out of the question—come on, it meant eternal damnation—I had to convince myself that the behavior was necessary, that it was for my own good. But after meeting with the Presbyterian minister, I no longer felt compelled to deny the evidence against what I had been taught. I had permission to look objectively at *all* of the evidence and let my heart and mind decide what I really believed, and then reconcile my behavior with my "new" beliefs. I grew up in an Assembly of God church (one that a Presbyterian might find refreshingly emotional!)—but I could have picked up a self-righteous cloak from any church or religion.

The Catholic Church recently paid out $200 million to 144 people who claimed they were sexually abused by clergy members, clergy members who wanted to be "good." And they are. I'm not suggesting that they are "bad." I'm suggesting that they could not find their goodness in religion, and that what they found instead was a dead end. A lawyer for several plaintiffs said that the most important part of the case was having the church agree to release reams of personnel documents that are expected to chronicle the history and pattern of abuse. The individual plaintiffs also wanted to be "good." We all do and we all are.

But a church can't make us feel good enough any more than a book or a genie in a brass lamp can make us feel good enough. Even God can't make us feel good enough. He refuses to *make* us do anything. He created us good enough. And then he gave us the power to choose. We can only feel good enough by going within and realizing that we are innately good. Everything else is just a temporary fix or a coat of pretty paint for the outside.

After talking with my pastor, I had permission to look for the truth beyond the four walls of a church and the literal interpretation of the Bible. I read Marianne Williamson's *Return to Love,* which painted a poignant picture of what I innately knew love was. It took me back to my childhood when I tried to reconcile the behavior I saw in Christians with what I understood Jesus to say. Somehow I knew it wasn't loving for my mom to get so angry with my dad, no matter what he did (he was an unrepentant "sinner"—so I didn't expect righteousness from him). I knew that "Sister Fanning" at church who criticized my sister's culottes was not treating us the way Jesus would have, and yet she seemed to be doing it in Jesus's name. And it seemed to me that the minister's wife openly resented her husband's silly behavior, as though it was okay for her to feel bitter. *A Course in Miracles,* which Williamson based her book on, says:

> Only love is real.
> Nothing real can be threatened.
> Nothing unreal exists.
> Herein lies the peace of God.

> God is not the author of fear. You are.

1 John 4:18 of the Bible (New American Standard) says:

There is no fear in love; but perfect love casts out fear, because fear involves punishment, and the one who fears is not perfected in love.

It struck me that the Christian church at large had eventually developed a package of rules and regulations and offered them as an insurance policy instead of teaching us to trust the love that Jesus demonstrated, the same love that he said summed up the law (Matthew 22:37–40). It is easier to spell out and enforce dogma than love. It is easier to accept an insurance policy than it is to trust love enough to let go of everything else as Jesus taught.

And nobody could say it better than Jesus said it, "Up to the time of John it was the Law and the Prophets; since then, the kingdom of God has been preached, and by violence everyone is getting in" (Luke 16:16, Jerusalem Bible).

"The Law was a protection against a direct experience of the kingdom of God. By Fulfilling the Law, people hoped to achieve their proper relationship with God without having to relate to the inner world. But it was, as Nicholas Berdyaev said in *The Meaning of the Creative Act,* an ethic of obedience, not of creativity. The kingdom, however, is dynamically creative, and the ethic of the kingdom is a creative ethic based on consciousness and love, not on legalism. Now that the kingdom has come the old rigid outlook embodied in the Law will be violently assaulted so that the new and creative person may appear," says John A. Sanford in the respected classic *The Kingdom Within.*

Later I would learn that Thomas Jefferson, in about 1800, had taken scissors to the King James Bible (first published in 1611 after centuries of debate) to salvage Jesus's teachings in his own compilation, which he called *The Philosophy of Jesus of Nazareth*. He claimed to have rescued "the diamonds from the dunghill," by leaving the miracles the church used for their own purposes behind.

Ralph Waldo Emerson, in 1838, addressed the senior class of the Divinity College at Cambridge with, "He [Jesus] saw that God incarnates himself in man, and evermore goes forth anew to take possession of his world. He said, in this jubilee of sublime emotion, 'I am divine. Through me, God acts; through me, speaks. Would you see God, see me; or, see thee, when thou also thinkest as I now think.' But what a distortion did his doctrine and memory suffer in the same, in the next, and the following ages!"

"We have become so accustomed to the religious lie that surrounds us that we do not notice the atrocity, stupidity and cruelty with which the teaching of the Christian church is permeated," said Leo Tolstoy.

My own irreverence—and guts, as the case may be—paled in comparison to that of such respected, seasoned thinkers. Later I would read such scholarly works as *Beyond Belief: The Secret Gospel of Thomas* by Elaine Pagels, and her reverence would help me recognize my own, as well as Jefferson's, Emerson's, and Tolstoy's. It is the truth that we must reverence! Pagels writes, "When I found that I no longer believed everything I thought Christians were supposed to believe, I asked myself, Why not just leave Christianity—and religion—behind, as so many others have done? Yet I sometimes encountered, in churches and elsewhere—in the presence of a venerable Buddhist monk, in the cantor's singing at prayer services and on mountain hikes—something compelling, powerful, even terrifying that I could not ignore, and I had come to see that, besides belief, Christianity involves *practice*—and paths toward transformation."

The Gospel of Thomas, like the "gospel" laid out by Thomas Jefferson, presents Jesus as a teacher rather than a savior. Some would argue that the church needed a savior on which to build a church. And that is exactly what they voted on in 325 AD at the First Council of Nicaea, convoked by the Roman emperor Constantine I to resolve disagreements about the nature of Jesus. Thus, we have the Nicene Creed:

We believe in one God the Father Almighty, Maker of heaven and earth, and of all things visible and invisible. And in one Lord Jesus Christ, the only-begotten Son of God, begotten of the Father before all worlds, God of God, Light of Light, Very God of Very God, begotten, not made, being of one substance with the Father by whom all things were made; who for us men, and for our salvation, came down from heaven, and was incarnate by the Holy Spirit and the Virgin Mary, and was made man, and was crucified also for us under Pontius Pilate. He suffered and was buried, and the third day he rose again according to the Scriptures, and ascended into heaven, and sitteth on the right hand of the Father. And he shall come again with glory to judge both the quick and the dead, whose kingdom shall have no end. And we believe in the

Holy Spirit, the Lord and Giver of Life, who proceedeth from the Father who with the Father and the Son together is worshipped and glorified, who spoke by the prophets. And we believe in one holy catholic and apostolic Church. We acknowledge one baptism for the remission of sins. And we look for the resurrection of the dead, and the life of the world to come. Amen.

The truth cannot be found in fear; it can only be found in love. I have found the truth—not in a book, not in a university, or in a church, but in the deep recesses of my soul. And that is where Jesus, and any great teacher, would have us find it.

"For whoever has not known himself knows nothing, but whoever has known himself has simultaneously come to know the depth of all things," said Jesus (Book of Thomas the Contender, one of the ancient books discovered at Nag Hammadi).

"It is certainly hard to change one's set opinions, but a man should let himself freely test all philosophical systems, adopting and rejecting them as he sees fit. He [the wise man] goes along his independent way," said Buddha. To those who accept Buddha's teachings, the rituals, offerings, prayer wheels, and similar methods to get supernatural help are of virtually no value. The value of prayer and homage is the state of mind we reach in practicing them. As Pagels said so well, "Besides belief, Christianity involves *practice*—and paths toward transformation." It is a path toward transformation that we look for in any religion. And only in finding that path—whatever it looks like for us—do we avoid the dead end.

CHAPTER SEVEN

Food

TELL ME WHAT YOU EAT,
AND I WILL TELL YOU WHAT YOU ARE.

—JEAN ANTHELME BRILLAT-SAVARIN

AMERICANS SPEND AN estimated $35 billion a year on weight-loss products, products that offer no proof of effectiveness or safety. We want to believe that there is a painless way to lose weight. My sister jokingly says, "I'll do anything to lose weight but stop eating." We can laugh at the truth, but it is still the truth for an alarming percentage of the population. They are not stupid. They are addicted. How else can we explain two thirds of the adult population being overweight and nearly one third being obese (National Institutes of Health statistics)—despite the $35 billion spent to drop those unwanted pounds?

Weight is invariably a factor in physical attraction. And while we could easily defend our fat, it's tough to pretend that we think it's attractive while we're spending so much of our money to lose it. If the bad news is that we *perceive* ourselves to be less attractive, the worse news is that we *are* less healthy. Overweight and obese individuals are at increased risk for many diseases and serious health conditions, and obesity is the second-leading cause of preventable death in the United States (Centers for Disease Control and Prevention).

Our physical health is only one aspect of our overall health, though. Sadly, overeating is fueled by our lack of self-worth. The diet cliché "I already messed up today, I'll start tomorrow" epitomizes how we feel about ourselves. Our hope in the diet readily gives way to our internal sense of "we're doomed." People are not eating simply to satisfy their hunger for food. They are eating as an escape. They are eating as a source of pleasure—with too few *other* pleasures in their lives. It's one thing to reward yourself with a hot fudge sundae on occasion, the way you might reward yourself with a new hat, but if you console yourself with food on a daily basis while struggling to lose weight, you likely have a weight problem and an addiction problem.

Some impressive honesty and insight from a reader:

The line in your newspaper column about eating for pleasure, and sometimes we have too few pleasures, hit me so hard I cried.

I am currently about 70 pounds over my ideal weight. I am fully aware why, that is, too much food and too little activity. I am also fully aware that I look disgusting. But sometimes I feel that food is the only thing I have in my life anymore. It's the only thing I haven't had to trade off. I have a high-stress job that leaves me emotionally drained, then I have to come home and be peppy and upbeat while I cook, clean up, and handle life's details for everybody else in the house. I used to love to read, to write poetry, and take long walks, but what woman with a family has time for that these days? Modern life is a treadmill that never stops. And if I do take some time for me, I just feel guilty and depressed. Food has become my pleasure, my self-expression, and yes, my rebellion. As I mentioned above, I know I look disgusting, but would I be any less disgusting if I was an alcoholic? Or a junkie? Or a gambling or shopping addict? Well, at least I would look better, and that's what counts these days, isn't it?

At one of my workshops, a woman had an "aha moment" when she realized that she ate to exercise control over *something*. Her husband controlled everything else (or so it seemed). He couldn't manage her weight, though. He had to live with the way *she* managed it—whether he liked it or not. And she happened to know he didn't like it. It was her way of saying, "Oh yeah? Take that!"

We might start out with good intentions. We're trying to be a good spouse or parent, or bring the family together, or relax and refuel the only way it seems like we can. But eventually it *is* the only way we can relax and refuel . . . only it takes more and more food to fill the tank, until finally there is no filling it, even temporarily. We live in a constant state of lack. We don't just need another fix; we need another "drug," or therapist, or something.

Overeating is not just a physical problem. When we're eating to satisfy a hunger that food can never satisfy, it's an emotional and spiritual problem. We can only feel good about ourselves by being true to ourselves, and part of that is eating well and exercising. But there's more immediate gratification in sitting down to a bowl of potato chips, putting one and then another and another into the mouth ("Nobody can eat just one" should get the truth-in-advertising award). It's consoling; as long as we're putting in another potato chip, it feels like everything's going to be okay—comfort food to the rescue. And it requires less effort than it does to go for a walk, take a piano lesson, or read a book. And it's so easy to watch television while we're bypassing what would truly satisfy us, body, mind, and spirit.

We don't need another diet. We need to learn what it means to eat to satisfy hunger. In her book *Traveling Mercies,* the wonderfully naked Anne Lamott shares her own experience of learning to feed herself:

> So for the next week, my assignment was to notice what it felt like when I was hungry. It was so strange. I was once again the world's oldest toddler. I walked around peering down as if to look inside my stomach, as if it was one of those old-fashioned front-loading washing machines with a window through which you

could see the soapy water swirling over your clothes. And I paid attention until I was able to isolate this feeling in my stomach, a gritchy kind of emptiness, like a rat was scratching at the door, wanting to be let in.

"Wonderful," Rita [her therapist] said, and then gave me my next assignment: first, to notice when I was hungry, and then— this blew my mind—to feed myself.

I practiced, and all of a sudden I was Helen Keller after she breaks the code for "water," walking around touching things, learning their names. Only in my case, I was discovering which foods I was hungry for, and what it was like to eat them. . . .

. . . I'd eat a little, stop when I was no longer hungry. "Want one more cookie?" I'd ask.

"No thanks," I'd say. "But maybe later. . . ."

Have you stopped asking yourself if you're hungry—and, maybe, just started looking at the clock to see if it was time to eat? Have you stopped asking yourself, "Do you want fries with that?" and let somebody else ask you—or tell you? It's so easy to pick a number three with a large drink (it comes with a large fries, too). You are hungry, after all; besides, it's the best value . . . and you'll only eat what you want, right? And then there's the fine-dining experience. It titillates our senses with complex flavors and exquisite presentation. We don't want it to end; we want to bask in it. And to end it abruptly without dessert seems a travesty. It *deserves* a proper ending!

And so it is that we get caught. The thing is that the more we feed our bodies, the more we feed our appetites, and the more it takes to satisfy them. Thus, a growing obesity epidemic is threatening the health of millions of Americans in the United States, according to the Centers for Disease Control and Prevention. Being overweight and physical inactivity account for more than 300,000 premature deaths each year in the United States, second only to tobacco-related deaths (our addictions are killing us). Obesity is an epidemic and should be taken as seriously as any infectious disease epidemic.

Still, I dare say that what drives the spending of billions of dollars on weight-loss products is not concern for health, but concern for appearance. Our appearance gets more priority than our health. It seems that even in the face of this epidemic, we are primarily motivated by our egos . . . until, of course, the epidemic hits home with the news of obesity-related health issues.

As is the case with other addictions, food may have to bring us to our knees before we stop. Here's another excerpt from Anne Lamott's *Traveling Mercies*:

> It is, finally, so wonderful to have learned to eat . . . that I'm not uncomfortable calling it a small miracle. A friend who does not believe in God says, "Maybe not a miracle, but a little improvement," but to that I say, Listen! You must not have heard me right: I couldn't feed myself! So thanks for your input, but I know where I was, and I know where I am now, and you just can't get here from there. Something happened that I had despaired would ever happen. It was like being a woman who has despaired of ever

getting to be a mother but who now cradles a baby. So it was either a miracle—Picasso said, "Everything is a miracle; it's a miracle that one does not dissolve in one's bath like a lump of sugar"—or maybe it was more a gift, one that required some assembly. But whatever it was, learning to eat was about learning to live—and deciding to live; and it is one of the most radical things I've ever done.

When we hit bottom and get back up again, we know what we are made of.

But before we hit the bottom, even before we get addicted, we can develop habits that don't serve us. If you find yourself offering food as a reward for getting a job done, or if you routinely eat popcorn when you go to a movie—whether you're hungry or not—beware. You don't have to order a number three. *Neither* do you have to forgo a burger. Just stop eating when you're not hungry anymore. Order a kid's meal, or *share* a number three. Yes, food is intended for our pleasure, but its primary purpose is to sustain us.

If you don't have a weight problem, you're in the minority! If you do, you can learn to eat all over again.

To be clear, I am not suggesting that you can't be overweight and attractive. I *know* you can be. But you want to be healthy and happy as well! If you're struggling with your weight, you're also struggling to do what you must do to be true to your values (to your truth, to love). You can only know self-esteem and peace by aligning with who you are.

CHAPTER EIGHT

Drugs/Alcohol

MAN SEEKS TO ESCAPE HIMSELF IN MYTH,
AND DOES SO BY ANY MEANS AT HIS DISPOSAL.
DRUGS, ALCOHOL, OR LIES. UNABLE TO WITHDRAW
INTO HIMSELF, HE DISGUISES HIMSELF.
LIES AND INACCURACY GIVE HIM A FEW
MOMENTS OF COMFORT.

—JEAN COCTEAU

THERE ARE STILL those who would make drugs a vehicle for a high, a good time, even enlightenment. But what drugs provide is not real. What they destroy is.

And because their destruction can be painfully obvious, the addiction to drugs may seem more real than other addictions. It's not. But people exhaust their resources and then spend money that they don't have to feed and treat drug addiction, often going through a revolving door for social services. While a few struggling with addiction make the headlines, thousands of others (without celebrity status) make their lives a living hell. The Office of National Drug Control Policy reports that during this past year illicit drug users were about sixteen times more likely than nonusers to report being arrested and booked for larceny or theft; more than fourteen times more likely to be arrested and booked for such offenses as driving under the influence, drunkenness, or liquor law violations; and more than nine times more likely to be arrested and booked on an assault charge.

I was thirtyish; I lived alone. The house was always as I left it, except on this day. I pulled into the garage and immediately noticed that my bike, instead of hanging from the bike hook on the wall, was lying in the middle of my parking spot. My eyes moved to the door leading from the garage into the foyer; it was ajar! And as I walked trepidly through the door and then the house, I found a discarded bank that used to be filled with coins, a panty drawer emptied on the floor, an oily nose smudge on my bathroom mirror. For the first time in my life, I called 9-1-1. The police filed a report and explained that, based on what was taken (jewelry and stereo equipment) for a quick sale, the crime was likely motivated by the need to buy drugs. Two days later, I called 9-1-1 again, this time from my bed. They stayed on the phone with me until a police officer arrived at my door. He did not find anybody peering through the windows or running through the woods; he spoke softly and kindly and told me that the culprit was unlikely to return, knowing that our awareness was heightened. The thief wanted drug money; he did not want to be caught. Eventually, things felt "normal" again, and I could lie in bed without hearing scary noises; but I did—contrary to my former philosophy—install an alarm system and obtain an insurance policy that went beyond the mandate of my mortgage holder.

We can conservatively conclude that drug addiction is a significant factor in law enforcement, court, corrections, social welfare, health care, and insurance costs. But as is the case with other social issues, drug addiction starts with the family and wreaks havoc there first. Financial cost doesn't begin to paint a picture of what it costs the people who are addicted, the families who love them, and those who cross their paths at the "wrong" time.

I gave a dear friend a long gold chain—when she didn't want a short chain to draw attention to her aging neck—with a gold heart made of roses hanging on it. She loved the necklace and wore it regularly, though other gold stayed in her jewelry box. The heart and the roses took on special meaning. She would get upset a number of times over the years when she thought she had lost it. Over and over, she would find it again; sometimes she wouldn't tell me that she'd misplaced it—or feared it stolen—until she'd already found it. Finally, though, it did disappear. Years later, she would tell me through tears that her grandson had confessed to taking it and selling it for drugs. She had begged him not to take *that*, and to tell her if he ever did, so that she could recover it.

My friend probably fixes dinner for her grandson at least once a week. She has been a second mother to him, almost since her youngest son Darrell got custody of him and his brother and sister following a divorce. Darrell has had his own horrific battles with drugs; *his* father, a recovered alcoholic himself, somehow helped him make it through and regain his sanity. And Darrell, with the strength of a grizzly bear and the tenderness of a teddy bear, is giving his three children all he's got. Often, it seems to fall far short.

Drug addiction is an escape from what *seems* overwhelming to what is overwhelming. It may start out with wanting to relax and "take the edge off," but if it were just an "edge," you'd be able to take it off. You can't. It seems that if a little *helps*, more might do the job. It doesn't. Over and over again, it doesn't. There is not enough to get the blasted edge off. It may also start off as an effort to fit in. Many get hooked while still in high school or while binge drinking in college, but trying to fit in doesn't stop with school. Others get hooked dealing with the pressures of earning a living or making a profit.

I remember when I was contemplating a promotion to sales that meant wining and dining the clients, my boss asked me (knowing I didn't drink more than a half a glass of wine) what I was going to do when somebody wanted to sit at the bar and drink. "I guess I'll let him and make sure he has a ride home," I said. But as it turned out, clients didn't drink much with me; I think my ginger ale and honest curiosity (coming from a girl in her twenties) about why they drank took the fun out of it. Invariably people were motivated by fear—chasing what they were afraid they missed *or* running from what they wanted to escape. It makes sense that a low opinion of self or a bruise to the ego often "drives" people to drink.

You might be wondering where that leaves social drinking—you know, the drinking we do just to be social or have fun or be one of the group. I don't believe in it. But come on, you must have seen that coming. When we're free of the ego, we aren't motivated by the need to fit in, and we're *already* having fun.

As is the case with all addictions, the first step toward recovery is to realize that you have a problem. That's not enough, though. The battle with drugs can't be fought until you are convinced that you have a problem that you cannot manage or control, a problem you cannot dabble in or revisit—without being consumed by it.

The fact that the hole we try to fill with drugs cannot be filled with fame or money is made sadly clear by people who have both. You can pick a star from this week's headlines going in or out of rehab, a star looking for something that he's not getting from the fame or the money or the "success." We do not have to be superstars to get the message or learn the lesson. We do not have to be geniuses to realize that drug addiction is not a problem we can manage or hide.

It *is* a problem we can overcome. We must. And we must start at the family level. We must learn when to be a grizzly bear and when to be a teddy bear. We must learn to love well, starting with ourselves. That means getting to know ourselves, showing respect for who we are, and responding to our needs. It is the job of a lifetime!

CHAPTER NINE

Sex/Romantic Love

REMEMBER THAT THE BEST RELATIONSHIP
IS ONE IN WHICH YOUR LOVE FOR EACH OTHER
EXCEEDS YOUR NEED FOR EACH OTHER.

—THE DALAI LAMA

"I CAN'T LIVE without you" is a sign of great need, not love.

Our society has never been so sexually liberated—or enslaved. We have an insatiable appetite for more and have demanded an ongoing stream of media on how to get it. We are not trying to satisfy our libido or an emotional need for romance. And, no, we are not just looking for *great sex* OR *great romance* (it's not that hard to conjure up). We keep looking for more or better because we think with the right slice of what we loosely label love, we will feel better about ourselves.

Sex is a natural way to consummate love, to love and be loved completely. It is some of God's best work. It paves the way for emotional vulnerability, and it transforms what could be uncomely parts into mysteriously beautiful and adored ones. It exercises and gratifies our bodies—and it makes babies to keep the species alive! But sex is also a biological need, and it is, according to Maslow, at the bottom of the hierarchy of needs, along with food, air, and water! It is not about to provide us with self-esteem.

Yet, that is often what we seek in sex and romantic love. We try to find self-worth in how desirable others find us (yes, I speak from experience) or how much seed we can sow. We mistake sex for love and get preoccupied with it—buying the idea that we are *supposed* to want it more than we actually do—while sacrificing the connectedness we really want. When we have the oneness of love, we also have the real prize of sex.

Oneness is more than a great romp in the sack; it is a melding of body, mind, and spirit. It is a deep connection, a knowing that regardless of what you're up against, you have a partner. It requires that you know and love who you are, so that you can share all of who you are with a partner. But that's exactly the kind of truth, the kind of work, we try to escape in sex. And when we can't get the sex we want firsthand (or simply don't want to make the effort), we seem to settle for getting it independently or vicariously.

How desperate do we have to be to sit in front of a TV screen week after week to see what the "desperate housewives" are going to do next? Apparently not desperate enough to do something about our own lives . . . or do we imagine that viewers lead satisfying sexual lives? And were we looking for sex in *Sex and the City* that we were unable or too scared or too lazy to find in our neck of the woods?

Sex sells everything from toothpaste to sailboats because we want sex. Or do we? About 23 percent of unmarried men and 32 percent of unmarried women report that they have not had sex in the last year. About 13 percent of married couples report that they have had sex only a few times in the last year, and 45 percent report that they have had sex a few times a month. If we *really* wanted sex, wouldn't we have it more often? The average American adult watches TV for four hours and thirty-five minutes every day (A. C. Nielsen Co.)—that translates to 365 times in the last year or 30 times a month for a lingering four hours and thirty-five minutes a pop! You see, there's some effort and risk in sex, even in the context of a committed relationship. The gratification we get from watching it on TV requires nothing of us—no physical exertion and no responsibility for our own satisfaction or our partner's. All we have to do is sit back and relax, and if it doesn't come off well, we can laugh at the poor pathetic characters on the screen. Can we be addicted to sex without actually indulging in it? Yes. Just as we can be addicted to porn.

We have fueled a $13-billion-dollar-a-year porn industry. "A spike in Internet-based porn sales the past few years underscores a thirst for adult content on the Internet that has yet to be fulfilled by large adult enterprises," says Frederick Lane III, a longtime industry observer and author of *Obscene Profits: The Entrepreneurs of Pornography in the Cyber Age*. The "plain brown wrappers" are no longer necessary. You have your own personal computer screen;

and you can protect your privacy with your own personal pass code. It's an all-you-can-eat buffet, and unless you're a real glutton, it's free. That doesn't mean you can get your fill, though, not when sex is an addiction, a means of filling a need with something that can never really fill it.

And likewise, we pursue romance—with more fervor and foolishness than any other animal in heat, because *we* are trying to meet more than a mere biological need. We are trying to live the happily-ever-after dream. If we can pull that off, then everything will be okay, or so we think. When we are under the spell of infatuation, it seems as though we have finally found oneness. We no longer feel separate and incomplete.

Somebody is interested in every word we have to say; they're watching our every move. They want to be with us every waking moment. At last somebody sees us for who we really are, in all of our glory. Well, sort of. What they really see is their own salvation—somebody who finally makes *them* feel good enough. And this is why infatuation is short-lived. Reality kicks in. Nobody else can save us. Infatuation feels so good, though, so absolutely incredible, that we go back for more—again and again and again! Despite the heart-wrenching pain of breaking up, despite our vows that we're through, we cannot resist trying our hand at "love" again when Cupid's arrow strikes. And, yes, we can get addicted to the high of infatuation, the newness, the insatiable desire.

We can also recognize it for what it is. We can give it a foundation of intimacy, but only by sharing who we really are with a partner. Only then can we connect on a deep level—mentally, emotionally, and spiritually. We must be willing to honestly open up and put ourselves out there, knowing that we might not be what somebody else is looking for, knowing that we could get rejected. But when we have come to know and thus love who we are, we are no longer daunted by somebody else's rejection! We no longer need the crazed state of infatuation to see greener grass and butterflies wafting through it. We can see smiles and wonder we missed before. We can feel—and be—more alive and get more done. We can be in that state of knowing that everything is okay; in fact, everything is just perfect. We can—if you will—be our own salvation!

We no longer *need* somebody else to come along and make us feel desirable or important. We know how desirable and important we are! There is no more pretending. And there is no need for a temporary fix from shallow sex or newness or even romantic dinners. We've got all the fix we need. Once we truly know who we are, it's impeccably clear that somebody else's opinion cannot change who we are—for better or worse! Our joy is no longer contingent on somebody else.

We are free . . . and awfully attractive to a healthy person!

CHAPTER TEN

Accomplishment/ Education/Notoriety

HE ALONE IS GREAT AND HAPPY WHO
REQUIRES NEITHER TO COMMAND NOR TO OBEY
IN ORDER TO SECURE HIS BEING OF SOME
IMPORTANCE IN THE WORLD.

—JOHANN WOLFGANG VON GOETHE

WHEN WE REALIZE our inner greatness, we can be sure of our importance (as well as our neighbor's). Until then, we seek somebody to lead us or follow us, so that we might be affirmed. Our seeking, though, unveils our insecurity. No matter who leads us, and no matter who follows us, *we* are the same. We cannot find worth in how we are received or in how we measure up to others.

In the "Desiderata," which is Latin for "desired things," Max Ehrmann advised:

If you compare yourself with others,
you may become vain and bitter;
for always there will be greater and lesser
persons than yourself.

As we become more informed of newsworthy accomplishments, our own lives can seem a little (or a lot) bleak. We have a window to the world on both computer and television screens. We can watch the rich and famous (or those taking a shot at rich and famous) at work and at play. We can pull up the Nobel Prize winner, the saint, the artist, the virtuoso, or the royal prince. And we can compare ourselves with all of them. Our comparisons, though, are largely based on what can be quantified. And what *cannot* be quantified in human beings is the same in each of us. Nonetheless, we tend to focus on, perhaps even get obsessed with, what we can measure. Today, more so than when Max Ehrmann penned the words in 1927, we can find reasons to be "vain and bitter."

We are compelled to do more and learn more, to stand out more. But are we just going through the motions, just playing a game? Do we really do more—or do we just take a promotion? Do we really know more—or do we just get a degree? Do we get more notable—or just spend more time getting press? "Money was never a big motivation for me, except as a way to keep score," says Donald Trump. "The real excitement is playing the game." It's not so much what we do as it is our motivation for doing it. We can write a book to share love or we can write a book to boost our ego—or one-up the next billionaire, as the case may be.

Anytime we do something from ego, we really do it from fear: fear of what others think, fear that there's not quite enough to go around, fear that we might lose our spot, fear that if we do, it will mean that *we* fall short. It's important to stop and examine our motivation—whether it's in pursuit of a career, an education, or a professional standing. Does reaching the goal serve *you* or your ego? Does it serve your family? Does it serve society? Is your life more or less loving as a result of reaching the goal?

I have a friend who went to school for computer science and earned a bachelor's degree. Then he went back to school and earned a degree in accounting. Not enough—he went back and got an MBA. Still not enough—he went back and got a law degree, or a Juris Doctor, as he preferred to call it. I think he wanted to be bigger than life, like Richard Gere in *Pretty Woman*. Clearly he wanted to marry a "Julia Roberts," and perhaps he thought that was the only way to win her heart. He was short, about 5'4". And while that may seem a conspicuous deficit to overcome, his insecurity (if I may be so bold) is no more or less well founded than yours or mine.

He used to tell me, as he surveyed my reading material—stuff like *The American Dictionary of Cultural Literacy*—that I was doing it the hard way. I was not about to go back to school just for a piece of paper that might win somebody else's approval. Nor was I about to be found wanting some piece of knowledge expected of the well learned. We were both trying to be "normal," both trying to be impressive, both trying to feel good enough. And we were both doing it the *hard* way!

A small business is no longer impressive; a four-year degree is no longer impressive. But once you have a *big* business or a Ph.D., those are no longer impressive either. And even the undeniably impressive can seem like a fluke or a stroke of luck—which we cling to, knowing we could never get that "lucky" twice. The *only thing* that remains impressive is that which we cannot see, that which we cannot boast of, that which is the same in all of us.

Think about somebody you used to be impressed with. Are you still? If what impressed you about the person was tangible, they have probably ceased to impress you. If it was intangible, they probably continue to impress you. And if you look inside *yourself,* you can find that intangible quality you admire. You will not find it in another job or a better school or more notoriety. Those are dead ends—perhaps bad habits or addictions—on the road to happiness. They are lit up by ego, which makes a lousy navigator. Nonetheless, it is our navigator until we have moved on to meet our need for self-esteem.

"It is impossible to escape the impression that people commonly use false standards of measurement—that they seek power, success and wealth for themselves and admire them in others, and that they underestimate what is of true value in life," said Sigmund Freud in his opening statement of *Civilization and Its Discontents.*

CHAPTER ELEVEN

Busyness

THE BEST WAY TO AVOID RESPONSIBILITY IS TO SAY,
"I'VE GOT RESPONSIBILITIES."

—RICHARD BACH

WE HAVE NEVER had so much leisure time or so many ways to fill it. The average American works five to eight hours less per week than in 1965. That might not sound dramatic, but if we took the extra leisure time all at once, we could take an additional five to ten weeks off per year!

It seems we prefer to fill the time up, though, even if it's in front of the TV—which is where the average American spends half of their leisure time. We spend some of the rest of it standing in line to shell out money for movies, sporting events, concerts, theme parks, plays, and security checks. We even pay to stand in line and use exercise equipment at the gym. People used to exercise at home and walk around the neighborhood. If you are as old as I am, perhaps you remember when going to the park was a treat. As a girl, I used to run to the top of the hills and lie down in the soft green grass, and then push off with one leg and roll down—only to run back up to the top of the hill and do it again. No skis, no snowboard, no snow!

Today, 8.7 percent of personal consumption is spent on recreation, up from 6.6 percent in 1970. The increase is more striking when you look at the dollars—we spend $2,500 per person on recreation each year, about three times the $850 spent in 1970. We have more leisure time and more money to spend on it. But we have never been so "busy."

Pat and Gary Nebel, my website experts, are award-winning nature photographers who spend weekends capturing the exquisite. And I'm always amazed at how untouched their destinations are. How is it that they have acres and acres of wildlife refuges almost entirely to themselves? While some of the most unique landscapes of this country are dedicated to parks with clean restrooms and free drinking water, fountains and waterfalls, ponds and gardens, forests and mountains, rivers and beaches, we choose theme parks instead. We pay $30 or $60 instead of $3, take a shuttle from the parking lot, and stand in line for hours rather than enjoy plenty of parking next to the gate with no wait. What exactly is our motivation?

It's easier for us to surround ourselves with people and busyness than nature and solitude. It's easier for us to talk about a roller coaster or the latest technology than it is for us to try to describe a breathtaking view or articulate our appreciation of a garden. We feel more important going to see somebody famous in concert than sitting in an outdoor café with live music where we can actually look into the soul of the musician.

So it is that we spend our time, money, energy, and, in some cases, our health being entertained or busied. Maybe you prefer to participate. Maybe you play softball or swim on a team. Maybe you're always making "improvements" around the house or the yard. Maybe you shop for the house, the family, gifts, that hard-to-find piece of art. Maybe you serve the kids, the neighborhood, the church, the school. We can use productive projects, fine entertainment, or service to others to busy ourselves, or escape what we do not want to face.

We leave little time for contemplative thought or soul-searching. Our biggest challenge is to be still! *That* could bring us face-to-face with what we run from. Ironically, what we run from—the truth of who we are—is also what we seek.

The outcry seems to be, "I don't have time for me." But the truth is, "I don't take time for me." If you're an exception and you take time to care for yourself in a way that feels healthy to you, wonderful! But if you can't seem to find time to eat right or learn what you want to know or practice what you already know, *stop* and *take* the time to look at what you're doing instead and why. When we don't really want to take care of ourselves, it's easy to find reasons or excuses not to. If you've wanted to organize your closet for the last six months—or six years—and you haven't quite gotten to it, chances are, you don't *really* want to organize your closet, not as much as you want to avoid it. And when you want to avoid something, you can *find* a reason. You really should take the kids to the new theme park, or you really should visit your parents. "Should" is a yellow flag; often it helps us justify avoiding or postponing what we don't want to tackle.

We tend to prioritize based on our emotions (all the negative ones being rooted in fear) and then justify our priorities with would-be logic. Maybe you don't exercise because you don't *feel* like exercising. Rather than admit that to yourself and deal with why you don't want to exercise, you reason that it's not as important as going to a movie with your husband. You really *should* spend some time together. So, you put off exercising, over and over again, not just for a few days. We might be talking years, minus the twelve days you put in along the way.

Maybe you've learned that if you take Suzie to piano and Johnny to soccer that you don't have to worry about you. (If you're asking who will take Suzie and Johnny if you don't, you might also ask who will take care of you if you don't.) If you work Monday through Friday and you're too tired for anything but television at night, and you spend weekends on errands and the yard and the boat, then you're off the hook. You don't have time for you. And that becomes your ongoing excuse for neglect.

"I thought that what I was afraid of more than anything else was that something awful would happen to them, but the secret I began to glimpse was that I was really less afraid for the children than I was afraid for myself. What awful thing would happen to me if something happened to them—that was what I was afraid of. What dangerous and unknown new role might I fall into if the role of father were taken from me and suddenly the sky was the limit, if instead of trying to take care of my children's needs, I started taking care of my own needs, some of which were so powerful and long neglected that I was afraid they might overwhelm me?" says Frederick Buechner in *Telling Secrets,* his wonderfully rich memoir.

I know, some of you feel guilty for taking time for yourselves. That's precisely what you need to look at. Why do you feel guilty? Or perhaps a better question is: why do you feel unworthy? When you realize that you're choosing to busy yourself, you will begin to understand why you get busier and busier and busier without ever getting it all done. The good news is: You're worthy! You are innately good.

And you can't love somebody else any better than you can love yourself.

Part Three

The Truth—
We Are Innately Good

As long as we think we are
the ego, we feel attached and fall
into sorrow. But realize that you
are the Self, the Lord of life, and
you will be freed from sorrow.
When you realize that you are the
Self, supreme source of light,
supreme source of love, you
transcend the duality of life and
enter into the unitive state.

—The Upanishads

YOUR EGO IS not who you are; it is not your true self. It is not your opinion of yourself; it is your *defense* of what you think of yourself. It is what you project to others to be acceptable. Inevitably, though, putting our ego out front leads to disappointment or sorrow. But having decided that there is something wrong with us, we are afraid to look at the depth of our flaw or our pain. Ironically, the truth we fear (the truth of who we are) is the very truth we long for, the very truth that will set us free. "Have confidence in the truth, although you may not be able to comprehend it, although you may suppose its sweetness to be bitter, although you may shrink from it at first. Trust in the Truth. . . . Have faith in the Truth and live it," said Buddha.

Until we trust the truth, we cling to our ego, or security blanket, that which we use to win acceptance and approval from others (or even God). It is only when we let go of the ego and whatever temporary gratification it offers us that we are able to embrace the life of love we want. We cannot truly uncover the love within until we let go of what hides it. It's not that we can't have all the niceties that money and status afford us and still have a life of love; it's that we can't *cling* to the niceties and still have a life of love. Paradoxically, once we align our behavior with the love within, the niceties we have let go of are well within our reach, but they are forevermore insignificant.

The truth is always beautiful, and when we finally look at it, we see the love within us. We recognize it as the feeling we get when we see a baby against his mother's breast, or the first green of a green bean plant peeking through dark soil, or a crescent moon suspended in the night sky. We are awed by our divinity. What we thought was paradise was really a prelude from a purely instinctual animal existence to a conscious awareness. Going back is not an option. The force that wanted us to know the difference between good and evil is a good force, and it made *us* good. With the power of good, we are everything we always wanted to be. We are not responsible for creating our goodness, only choosing to live it.

And by choosing goodness, we light the darkness; we let go of fear and its entourage of negative emotion. There is no darkness where light dwells. There is no fear where love dwells. One displaces the other. They *cannot* coexist.

And you are the light; you are the love.

CHAPTER TWELVE

Evil Is an Alternative, Not Our Nature

TRUST YOURSELF, THEN YOU WILL
KNOW HOW TO LIVE.

—JOHANN WOLFGANG VON GOETHE

THE ONLY WAY to be happy is to be true to yourself. The only way to be unhappy is to be untrue to yourself. Why can't we simply trust our nature enough to be true to it and live happily ever after? We can.

But first we must really look at who we are. At a core level, we are love, and there is nothing more trustworthy. We are afraid to look too far beneath the surface, though. We can't look while we are clinging to the ego, or our security blanket, which hides our true self. Over and over again, I have looked into the eyes of earnest people telling me that they don't know who they are. Maybe they started taking care of a family twenty years ago. Maybe they went to work as a doctor, or a service technician, or

121

a secretary right out of school. Maybe they're still floundering, not knowing *what* to do.

We are *told*—in so many words and nods and prods—who we are before we discover ourselves, and once we buy into a false notion, we tend to hold on to it. So, it's not that we aren't trying to be who we are; it just turns out that we're trying to be some image conjured up by our egos. *We* are lost beneath the layers designed to make us what we think we are supposed to be, what we are afraid we're not. "This above all else: To thine own self be true, and it must follow, as the night the day, thou canst not then be false to any man," said William Shakespeare. Likewise, if we're *not* being true to ourselves, we are not being true to *anybody*.

From the Beginning

From the beginning, man has had to forge a survival, and he has in that process sought to know how and why he came to be, how and why he should live, and how and why he would die. He has sought meaning in heaven and earth, the wind and rain and fire. He would attribute what he did not understand and what he could not control to the gods. Finding himself at their mercy, he would fear, worship, and try to appease them. He would construe reward and punishment in their response and strive harder to find favor with them—both the just and the unjust.

Many centuries would come and go before man (or at least some men) would consolidate his multiple gods and trust God to be benevolent and just. It would not happen until man shifted his focus inward to see his own potential for goodness and realized that goodness was its own reward. As long as man was coming from ego, he framed God through an egoic mind.

According to a theory by German philosopher Karl Jaspers, during 800 BC–200 BC, what he called the "axial age," people of the Western world, China, and India reached a pivotal point, not forsaking ritual, but making ritual a more personal experience. They realized that each individual had to experience religion for himself, and, that in doing so, he would see both his value and his neighbor's, eventually finding unity or oneness. Thus, we had several versions of the golden rule—best known as "Do unto others as you would have them do unto you"—before Jesus ever said, "Love your neighbor as you love yourself" (Matthew 22:39): "What is hateful to you, do not to your fellowmen. That is the entire Law; all the rest is commentary" (Talmud); "Do not do to others what you would not like yourself" (Confucius); "This is the sum of duty: Do naught unto others which would cause you pain if done to you" (Mahabharata); "That nature alone is good which refrains from doing unto another whatsoever is not good for itself" (Zoroastrianism). And while we have complicated the message, the message remains in all major religions: Hinduism, Confucianism, Taoism, Buddhism, Judaism, Christianity, Islam, and also the primal religions. And to obey the golden rule means to:

1. Know who we are

2. Love who we are

3. Know our neighbor

4. Love our neighbor

If you accomplish number one, you will also accomplish numbers two, three, and four. To know you is to love you. To know you is to know your neighbor. And to know your neighbor is to love your neighbor. Oneness, another common thread in the major religions, follows. That's why I'm writing this book—if I can help you to know yourself, the rest follows. Jesus said, "Seek first the kingdom of God and his righteousness, and all other things will be yours as well," (Matthew 6:33). He also said, "The kingdom of God is within you," (Luke 17:21). So, who are you? What is your nature? Why is knowing such a struggle?

An old Cherokee was teaching his grandson about life. "There is a fight going on inside of me," he said to the boy.

"It is a terrible fight and it is between two wolves. One is evil—he is anger, envy, sorrow, regret, greed, arrogance, self-pity, guilt, resentment, inferiority, lies, false pride, superiority, and ego. The other is good—he is joy, peace, love, hope, serenity, humility, kindness, benevolence, empathy, generosity, truth, compassion, and faith.

"This same fight is going on inside you—and inside every other person, too."

The grandson thought about it for a minute and then asked his grandfather, "Which wolf will win?"

The old Cherokee simply replied, "The one you feed."

You have an awareness of the two wolves, but you are *not* the two wolves. They represent your conscience, or your knowledge of good and evil. You are good. Evil is not your nature; it is an alternative. To choose good is to trust love; to choose evil is to yield to fear. You cannot choose love *and* fear. When you choose love, it displaces fear; when you choose fear, it displaces love. You cannot *kill* love, though; you cannot kill the good wolf. He will always remain, even if buried beneath the weight of the evil wolf. "But we are all born between urine and feces, and even in the most degraded among us, the innocence we once came from is still somewhere alive. Beneath all our pain and delusions and unsatisfied desires, it shines with its pristine light, as it did in the beginning," says Stephen Mitchell in *The Gospel According to Jesus.*

Americanized Christianity makes it easy to lose sight of the fact that Christianity is rooted in mysticism. It cannot *really* grow into something else. The orange seed cannot grow a plum tree or bear plums. A dear friend and missionary, Mary Ann Hastings, told me, "Christianity must return to mysticism." At first she took me by surprise—I was only beginning to learn that my Christianity *had* roots in mysticism—what she took for granted was still new to me. Her matter of fact attitude, as an *Assembly of God* missionary, helped me realize that my trepidation was unnecessary. Of course it was—it was rooted in fear. Smile. But now, years later, her words and the truth ring even more clearly.

Mysticism, according to *Webster's*, is: "The experience of mystical union or direct communion with ultimate reality reported by mystics; the belief that direct knowledge of God, spiritual truth, or ultimate reality can be attained through subjective experience (as intuition or insight)." It makes sense, then, that Christian mystics have a deep knowing based on their own experience of God that frees them to interpret sacred texts through the light of love, rather than dogma.

You probably learned that you were innately bad or in need of salvation—or at least doomed to wrestle with a dual nature. You may have learned it from an account of creation in Genesis, the first book of both the Christian Bible and the Jewish Torah. And you may have been taught to view it as the divinely inspired Word of God or as a myth. Both of those are intended to help us find meaning in life. I include one of the accounts of creation below, because although it may play a significant role in your thinking, that role may be based on what you read, or only heard, many years ago. Perhaps you'll read it now without the bias of fear—yours, a parent's, a well-meaning teacher's, or a minister's. You can trust the truth—whatever it is—to resonate.

In the beginning God created the heavens and the earth.

Now the earth was formless and empty, darkness was over the surface of the deep, and the Spirit of God was hovering over the waters.

And God said, "Let there be light," and there was light. God saw that the light was good, and He separated the light from the darkness. God called the light "day," and the darkness he called "night." And there was evening, and there was morning—the first day.

And God said, "Let there be an expanse between the waters to separate water from water." So God made the expanse and separated the water under the expanse from the water above it. And it was so. God called the expanse "sky." And there was evening, and there was morning—the second day.

And God said, "Let the water under the sky be gathered to one place, and let dry ground appear." And it was so. God called the dry ground "land," and the gathered waters he called "seas." And God saw that it was good.

Then God said, "Let the land produce vegetation: seed-bearing plants and trees on the land that bear fruit with seed in it, according to their various kinds." And it was so. The land produced vegetation: plants bearing seed according to their kinds and trees bearing fruit with seed in it according to their kinds. And God saw that it was good. And there was evening, and there was morning—the third day.

And God said, "Let there be lights in the expanse of the sky to separate the day from the night, and let them serve as signs to mark seasons and days and years, and let them be lights in the expanse of the sky to give light on the earth." And it was so. God made two great lights—the greater light to govern the day and the lesser light to govern the night. He also made the stars. God set them in the expanse of the sky to give light on the earth, to govern the day and the night, and to separate light from darkness. And God saw that it was good. And there was evening, and there was morning—the fourth day.

And God said, "Let the water teem with living creatures, and let birds fly above the earth across the expanse of the sky." So God created the great creatures of the sea and every living and moving thing with which the water teems, according to their kinds, and every winged bird according to its kind. And God saw that it was good. God blessed them and said, "Be fruitful and increase in number and fill the water in the seas, and let the birds increase on the earth." And there was evening, and there was morning—the fifth day.

And God said, "Let the land produce living creatures according to their kinds: livestock, creatures that move along the ground, and wild animals, each according to its kind." And it was so. God made the wild animals according to their kinds, the livestock according to their kinds, and all the creatures that move along the ground according to their kinds. And God saw that it was good.

Then God said, "Let us make man in our image, in our likeness, and let them rule over the fish of the sea and the birds of the air, over the livestock, over all the earth, and over all the creatures that move along the ground."

So God created man in his own image, in the image of God he created him; male and female he created them.

God blessed them and said to them, "Be fruitful and increase in number; fill the earth and subdue it. Rule over the fish of the sea and the birds of the air and over every living creature that moves on the ground."

Then God said, "I give you every seed-bearing plant on the face of the whole earth and every tree that has fruit with seed in it. They will be yours for food. And to all the beasts of the earth and all the birds of the air and all the creatures that move on the ground—everything that has the breath of life in it—I give every green plant for food." And it was so.

God saw all that he had made, and it was very good. And there was evening, and there was morning—the sixth day.

Thus the heavens and the earth were completed in all their vast array.

By the seventh day God had finished the work he had been doing; so on the seventh day he rested from all his work. And God blessed the seventh day and made it holy, because on it he rested from all the work of creating that he had done.

(Genesis 1:1–2:3, New International Version)

Genesis offers an explanation of our existence, sustenance, and procreation. And, God deemed us very good and offered us his blessing! What happened!?

If you believe that the creation story above is to be taken literally, you may find another interpretation of the story heretical. Yet Genesis itself gives us another version of the story, one that many of us bought into, perhaps, without even questioning the many contradictions between the two stories. And it's interesting to note that heresy originally meant act of choice.

This is the account of the heavens and the earth when they were created.

When the LORD God made the earth and the heavens—and no shrub of the field had yet appeared on the earth and no plant of the field had yet sprung up, for the LORD God had not sent rain on the earth and there was no man to work the ground, but streams came up from the earth and watered the whole surface of the ground—the LORD God formed the man from the dust of the ground and breathed into his nostrils the breath of life, and the man became a living being.

Now the LORD God had planted a garden in the east, in Eden; and there he put the man he had formed. And the LORD God made all kinds of trees grow out of the ground—trees that were pleasing to the eye and good for food. In the middle of the garden were the tree of life and the tree of the knowledge of good and evil.

A river watering the garden flowed from Eden; from there it was separated into four headwaters. The name of the first is the Pishon; it winds through the entire land of Havilah, where there is gold. (The gold of that land is good; aromatic resin and onyx are also there.) The name of the second river is the Gihon; it winds through the entire land of Cush. The name of the third river is the Tigris; it runs along the east side of Asshur. And the fourth river is the Euphrates.

The LORD God took the man and put him in the Garden of Eden to work it and take care of it. And the LORD God commanded the man, "You are free to eat from any tree in the garden; but you must not eat from the tree of the knowledge of good and evil, for when you eat of it you will surely die."

The LORD God said, "It is not good for the man to be alone. I will make a helper suitable for him."

Now the LORD God had formed out of the ground all the beasts of the field and all the birds of the air. He brought them to the man to see what he would name them; and whatever the man called each living creature, that was its name. So the man gave names to all the livestock, the birds of the air and all the beasts of the field.

But for Adam no suitable helper was found. So the LORD God caused the man to fall into a deep sleep; and while he was sleeping, he took one of the man's ribs and closed up the place with flesh. Then the LORD God made a woman from the rib he had taken out of the man, and he brought her to the man.

The man said, "This is now bone of my bones and flesh of my flesh; she shall be called 'woman,' for she was taken out of man."

For this reason a man will leave his father and mother and be united to his wife, and they will become one flesh.

The man and his wife were both naked, and they felt no shame.

Now the serpent was more crafty than any of the wild animals the LORD God had made. He said to the woman, "Did God really say, 'You must not eat from any tree in the garden'?"

The woman said to the serpent, "We may eat fruit from the trees in the garden, but God did say, 'You must not eat fruit from the tree that is in the middle of the garden, and you must not touch it, or you will die.'"

"You will not surely die," the serpent said to the woman. "For God knows that when you eat of it your eyes will be opened, and you will be like God, knowing good and evil."

When the woman saw that the fruit of the tree was good for food and pleasing to the eye, and also desirable for gaining wisdom, she took some and ate it. She also gave some to her husband, who was with her, and he ate it. Then the eyes of both of them were opened, and they realized they were naked; so they sewed fig leaves together and made coverings for themselves.

Then the man and his wife heard the sound of the LORD God as he was walking in the garden in the cool of the day, and they hid from the LORD God among the trees of the garden. But the LORD God called to the man, "Where are you?"

He answered, "I heard you in the garden, and I was afraid because I was naked; so I hid."

And he said, "Who told you that you were naked? Have you eaten from the tree that I commanded you not to eat from?"

The man said, "The woman you put here with me—she gave me some fruit from the tree, and I ate it."

Then the LORD God said to the woman, "What is this you have done?" The woman said, "The serpent deceived me, and I ate."

So the LORD God said to the serpent, "Because you have done this, Cursed are you above all the livestock and all the wild animals! You will crawl on your belly and you will eat dust all the days of your life. And I will put enmity between you and the woman, and between your offspring and hers; he will crush your head, and you will strike his heel."

To the woman he said, "I will greatly increase your pains in childbearing; with pain you will give birth to children. Your desire will be for your husband, and he will rule over you."

To Adam he said, "Because you listened to your wife and ate from the tree about which I commanded you, 'You must not eat of it,' Cursed is the ground because of you; through painful toil you will eat of it all the days of your life. It will produce thorns and thistles for you, and you will eat the plants of the field. By the sweat of your brow you will eat your food until you return to the ground, since from it you were taken; for dust you are and to dust you will return."

Adam named his wife Eve, because she would become the mother of all the living.

The LORD God made garments of skin for Adam and his wife and clothed them. And the LORD God said, "The man has now become like one of us, knowing good and evil. He must not be allowed to reach out his hand and take also from the tree of life and eat, and live forever." So the LORD God banished him from the Garden of Eden to work the ground from which he had been taken. After he drove the man out, he placed on the east side of the Garden of Eden cherubim and a flaming sword flashing back and forth to guard the way to the tree of life.
(Genesis 2:4–3:24, New International Version)

What Genesis Tells Us

Christians and Jews who believe the Bible to be the infallible word of God believe that Moses recorded the entire book of Genesis in ca. 1500 BCE. But many scholars believe that the first account of creation was recorded by an anonymous writer from the sixth century BCE based on an earlier myth, and that the second account of creation was recorded by a writer who preferred to call God Yahweh, the name used when he revealed himself to Moses, from as early as the tenth century BCE. Infallible word of God or myth, the book of Genesis was recorded many centuries after God, according to the stories, created the first man. And in either case, there is much more than a literal meaning to be gleaned from this account.

By the time Genesis was recorded, the Israelites were beginning to believe in one God but, nonetheless, both versions of the creation story were included in the book. Herein we have a clue. The writer(s) was not threatened by more than one account—of God or creation—and did not intend for us to take either account literally. We *cannot* take *both* literally. Yet the Catholic Church executed early scientists for teaching that the earth moved around the sun, in apparent conflict with Genesis. When we don't have the truth, what we do have can be threatened. But the truth is not threatened; rather it is confirmed by facts. "I do not feel obliged to believe that the same God who has endowed us with sense, reason, and intellect has intended us to forgo their use," said Galileo Galilei, the Italian physicist and astronomer credited with the invention of the telescope and who proved that the earth revolves around the sun.

God was not threatened by the truth the way those who placed Galileo under house arrest must have been. It was only in 1992, 350 years after Galileo's death and three years after his namesake was launched to Jupiter, that the Vatican formally and publicly cleared Galileo of any wrongdoing. Pope John Paul II is on record as saying, "Galileo sensed in his scientific research the presence of the Creator who, stirring in the depths of his spirit, stimulated him, anticipating and assisting his intuitions."

And while it would be easy to leap to the conclusion that the church has learned a lesson, it would, indeed, be a *leap*. Since 1859 when Darwin published his *Origin of Species,* scientific evidence has mounted supporting the evolution of man as we know him over the last 150,000 years. Yet as recently as June 2007, 39 percent of the respondents to a USA Today/Gallup Poll said that the following statement of creationism was definitely true; and 27 percent of the respondents said it was probably true: "Creationism—that is, the idea that God created human beings pretty much in their present form at one time within the last 10,000 years."

Some of what we have learned, perhaps as fact, is really myth . . . and it was not initially intended to be presented as factual. Genesis is a perfect example of that. Had the recorder(s) of Genesis intended to present a historical account of creation, he wouldn't have presented two conflicting stories. He wasn't expecting us to not notice or pretend that we didn't! The timing, the sequence, the means of creation are all different, and only one of them includes disobedience or "sin."

St. Augustine didn't develop his doctrine of original sin until the fifth century CE. And while Jews believe in the duality of human nature, they do *not* believe that we are born into sin, and neither do the Eastern Orthodox Christians. "This only have I found: God made mankind upright, but men have gone in search of many schemes," said the author (whose identity is debated) of Ecclesiastes, a book in both the Jewish and the Christian Scriptures.

Man—as we know him—has always sought to understand his existence, his environment, good, and evil, and thus his creator. The story of creation, based on genealogies listed in Genesis, takes place about 3,000–4,000 years ago and explains night and day, water and land, plants and animals, as well as man's origin. Most scientists agree that the earth has been here for about 4.5 billion years and that man has been here in some form for about 150,000 years. The story could represent man's evolving from beast to human. We have, to my knowledge, no historical record of developing a conscience, or an awareness of good and evil, or a concept of morality. But in *The Origin of Consciousness in the Breakdown of the Bicameral Mind,* Julian Jaynes, a professor of psychology at Princeton, argued that ancient peoples were not conscious as we consider the term today, and that the change of human thinking occurred over a period of centuries about three thousand years ago. I don't know (of course, I don't) if we developed an awareness of good and evil as we evolved physically—or if we were, somewhere along the way, instilled with the awareness. I believe it to be a blessing, though, and not a curse. I believe it to make us human, and not evil.

Demonstrating Our Goodness

Regardless of how we see Genesis (fact or myth), apparently even after God himself declared that we were very good, our goodness had to be tested. Goodness when dictated is no longer goodness. Goodness is demonstrated by choice. Surely the God who could speak the earth into existence (regardless of how long it took him) could have programmed us to obey without question. He did not want robots—or even animals—with no capacity to choose evil (or to "sin") and no capacity to choose good either. From the beginning he intended for us to choose. And I have to believe that he anticipated the inherent struggle of choice.

Take away choice, and what you have left is only blind obedience, and that's different from obedience by choice, different from goodness, and, therefore, different from love. Take away choice, and there is no love.

According to Genesis, our first choice was to obey God and not eat of the tree of the knowledge of good and evil *or* to be lured by something good to eat that was pleasing to the eye and able to open our eyes and make us like God. There was plenty of other fruit that was good to eat and pleasing to the eye, so those qualities only served to justify our disobedience. I liken this story to a parent leaving his two toddlers in their playroom and telling them not to touch the shiny red slide in the middle of the room, all the while knowing that the crafty child from next door was standing under the slide rehearsing a little sales pitch. God could not truly give us a choice without creating a reasonably attractive option.

And we could not choose "good" before acquiring the knowledge of good and evil. God had to equip us with the knowledge of good and evil (whether it was through a piece of fruit or a falling star or eons of evolution), for us to demonstrate our goodness.

Demonstrating our goodness would not be easy, though. We would act like the immature children we were. That does not mean that we surprised the God of the universe! Before Adam was cursed with working the ground, Genesis says, "When the LORD God made the earth and the heavens—and no shrub of the field had yet appeared on the earth and no plant of the field had yet sprung up, for the LORD God had not sent rain on the earth and there was no man to work the ground. . . ." Apparently God anticipated Adam working the ground (did he initially intend it to be easier?), and I believe he also anticipated Eve's travail in giving birth (we are not the only animals to labor for food and babies). So, while *we* may have been horrified on first reading how Cain, Adam and Eve's firstborn son, killed Abel, their second son, I suspect God understood from the beginning that we would learn what seems the hard way to choose good over evil.

As we continue to watch men and women in the Bible, they do learn the value of aligning their choices with God, with love, with their essence, with everything good. And we can learn from their lessons. Seeing men of courage and stature stumble and fall, sometimes in hideous ways, helps us to realize that falling down—and getting up again—is part of learning.

The falling doesn't make us bad; it makes us human. Perhaps the most ideal picture of perfection is a newborn baby. We look on in awe at how an egg fertilized nine months earlier can grow into a baby and emerge from its mother's womb breathing and crying and squirming and sleeping. Even those who don't believe in God have a sense of the miraculous and the divine in those first moments and days of birth. The tiny baby is perfect! We see no flaw in him. And as he grows in strength and awareness and curiosity, he begins to crawl and then to walk—or stumble as the case may be. Still looking on, we encourage and prod him; we hold his tiny fingers and help him to take those first steps. Inevitably, though, he falls. And when he does, he is still perfect. And so are we.

What we see over and over again in the Bible are men who stumble and fall, and men who run away from their "sin," even after repentance. But they can never really escape their deeds, just as we cannot escape our knowledge of good and evil, that which makes us human, that which allows us to be "good." In Genesis, after Jacob cunningly exchanged lentil stew for his famished brother Esau's birthright, he (with the help of their mother) tricked their father Isaac into blessing him as he would have blessed Esau as the firstborn son. The blessing was to mean fertility, wealth, and power. It did. But first Jacob would run for his life and reap the trickery he sowed: he would arrive at his uncle's house and work seven years for Rachel, the beautiful young woman he instantly fell in love with, and wake up with Leah, her older sister, instead. He would work another seven years for Rachel! His love for her would live on, but it would tear away at his wives and their children . . . and his heart. Nonetheless, Jacob "grew exceedingly rich, and had large flocks, and male and female slaves, and camels and donkeys."

Neither time nor blessing, though, would bring Jacob peace. He had hit a "dead end." Twenty years after the lentil stew, Jacob would, with trepidation, confront his fear and find his way back to his brother Esau. En route, he would dispatch a huge gift of livestock to Esau with the message that his servant Jacob was behind them. Esau "ran to meet him [Jacob] and embraced him, and fell on his neck and kissed him, and they wept."

It's interesting to note that Jacob and his mother Rebecca got in a hurry and seized control of the firstborn son's blessing. Had they left it to God, Jacob may well have received the blessing without their sowing all the trickery. Jacob's older brother Esau had disqualified himself from inheritance by marrying local Hittite women. And their father Isaac would have presumably known this, since it had been a condition of his own inheritance that he choose a wife from his father's family.

There is no peace without being true to who we are. Only in facing our own fears and reconciling with ourselves can we reconcile with others, with God. There is only one way to realize self-verification, and that is to align with our essence; and there is no way to feel good about ourselves *without* self-verification. *If we were innately evil, we would realize self-verification by aligning with evil.*

When Jesus was accused of casting out demons by Beelzebub, the ruler of the demons, he told his accusers that any kingdom divided against itself would be laid waste, and that any city or house divided against itself would not stand. He said, "If Satan casts out Satan, he is divided against himself; how then will his kingdom stand?" (Mark 3:22–26). If *we* were divided against ourselves, we could not stand, and a just God would not expect us to stand. We are innately good. Evil is not our nature—and it is not half of our nature—it is an alternative.

A scientist, God did not leave our goodness to chance. An artist, he contrasted good with evil, certainty with mystery. And choice is the life he breathed into his creation. A master artisan gives life to his work. He wants the "blood" to show; he wants what is inside to show through the exterior skin. Whether the object is a grape or a human being, it is more than skin-deep on the canvas. The juice, the anger, the compassion, the fear bleed through. And I believe God knew that our goodness—or love, the juice of all juice—would reveal itself as his creation evolved.

In Hinduism, that "juice" or spirit is the inner spiritual nature, the Universal Self or Atman, which is none other than Brahman, the concept of the supreme spirit, the unchanging, infinite, immanent, and transcendent reality. From the Hindu Upanishads:

Kena Upanishad: *Brahman, The Spirit: Not What People Here Adore*

What cannot be spoken with words, but that whereby words are spoken: Know that alone to be Brahman, the Spirit; and not what people here adore.

What cannot be thought with the mind, but that whereby the mind can think. . . .

What cannot be seen with the eye, but that whereby the eye can see. . . .

What cannot be heard with the ear, but that whereby the ear can hear. . . .

What cannot be indrawn with breath, but that whereby breath is indrawn: Know that alone to be Brahman, the Spirit; and not what people here adore.

"The most beautiful thing we can experience is the mysterious. It is the source of all true art and all science. He to whom this emotion is a stranger, who can no longer pause to wonder and stand rapt in awe, is as good as dead: his eyes are closed," said Albert Einstein. Our true self is that which transcends the ego, that which cannot be seen or heard or touched, that which is the source of everything that can be seen and heard and touched. Love.

CHAPTER THIRTEEN

Lighting Our "Darkness" to Let Go of Fear, False Beliefs, and All Negative Emotion

AT FIRST WE CANNOT SEE BEYOND
THE PATH THAT LEADS DOWNWARD TO DARK
AND HATEFUL THINGS—BUT NO LIGHT OR BEAUTY WILL
EVER COME FROM THE MAN WHO CANNOT BEAR THIS
SIGHT. LIGHT IS ALWAYS BORN OF DARKNESS, AND THE
SUN NEVER YET STOOD STILL IN HEAVEN TO SATISFY
MAN'S LONGING OR TO STILL HIS FEARS.

—CARL G. JUNG

WHEN WE SEE evil as a choice—and not our nature—we don't have to be afraid of ourselves or the dark. We can sit in solitude long enough to sense the doorway and begin the journey into darkness, which is really the journey into light. Because it is in the darkness that we learn to find our light.

"In the attitude of silence the soul finds the path in a clearer light. And what is elusive and deceptive resolves itself into crystal clearness. Our life is a long and arduous quest after truth," said Mahatma Gandhi. Until we light the path, we are bound to stumble. And, yes, we fall down. We curse the darkness, ourselves, and those around us; that is, until we realize that stumbling is a critical part of the plan—the learning part.

Our ongoing struggle to choose good does not make us bad. It makes us human; and what sets us apart from the animals is a gift. The problem is that we confuse our conscience (our recognition of evil and the inherent struggle of choice) with the indoctrination that we *are* evil or guilty or innately flawed, and while we may not verbalize that or even allow it into our consciousness, it is our ultimate fear, our ultimate pain. And it can be triggered, even when we have no conscious awareness of it.

I was strolling through an art festival when a painting got my attention. When I stopped to look, I started to cry. My first reaction was to pull my sunglasses out of my purse and hide my tears, but as I walked away, I realized that I had to go back. No other piece of art—apart from words (I'm a words girl from way back)—had ever made me cry. I had to own the painting. First, I would walk around and, inevitably, analyze what I felt. When I returned to buy the painting, the Chinese artist, in strained English, said, "I know you understand this one." She had seen my tears. Her husband, who spoke more fluent English, explained that his wife did the painting after working for days on her more thoroughly meticulous work. The pain deep inside me was triggered by the same pain that gushed from the artist when she needed to release it, and she knew I understood the pain.

The painting was a naked man (of course, I loved it) sitting on rocky ground, his head buried in his arms, his testicles just brushing the earth. It seemed he had been stripped of everything. He had nobody and nothing. He had stopped short, too weary to continue. But in the top left corner of the painting there was a sun, and scrawled inside the sun was a songbird, intended, according to Chinese legend, to send hope to the man. The hope had not broken through yet, but it would. And what had seemed impossible would be possible. When we reach a dead end and give up on salvation through something outside ourselves, we can find (with the help of a "songbird") the power of goodness, or love, within.

I *felt* the pain, but did I really understand it? I had been alone and weary of trying. I had felt drained by the task at hand, the task of being good enough, over and over again. Sometimes it was at work, when I wanted more money. Sometimes it was when I wanted to scream, because I couldn't seem to get along with or without somebody. Sometimes it was standing self-consciously in front of the mirror, not tall enough or pretty enough or *something* enough. Sometimes it was sitting in my car at a red light, hating myself for being late again. To *understand* the pain is to delve into the part we can't see, the darkness. The pain isn't *really* about money or pretty or being late. If it were, we could just shake ourselves with some well-chosen rational words: "Come on, you have a lot to be thankful for," or "You're overreacting—look at the big picture, this doesn't *really* matter."

Understanding Our Ultimate Fear

Maybe you're unaware of your pain, but it lurks behind your negative emotion—anger, control, resentment, blame. Before you can understand it, you have to feel it; you have to be willing to hurt instead of screaming or putting up a wall. "Love calls you to be brave," says my friend Michael. Once you feel your pain, to understand it, you have to ask yourself *why* it hurts. You'll be able to trace the pain to fear, and your ultimate fear is that there's something wrong with you. Think about it . . . why would it matter if you were late for an appointment if it didn't change how professional or courteous you were? Oh—they might think less of you, right? Well, would that matter, as long as you still knew the truth that you're really conscientious and thoughtful? Oh!—but, maybe, then, they wouldn't do business with you. But wait, would that matter if you knew you would always have just the right amount of business from just the right people? Would it matter if you had *any* business as long as you knew that you were doing what you loved, and that you were doing the best job you could do? Oh!—it wouldn't matter unless you went out of business? And why would that matter—unless somebody would think less of you? I have a friend who holds a master's degree and a prominent position and lives in a big, beautiful house who says, "As long as there's a McDonald's, I know I can find work." It's unlikely to come to that, but he knows it's okay if it does. He always gives his best!

If you knew that you were innately good, and that nobody

could ever do anything to take that away from you or change it, you would not have to worry about proving your goodness. You would not have to worry about whether there would be enough— of *whatever* you needed. You would not have to wonder if you would be happy. Your happiness and your peace would be unshakable—they would not be contingent on anything or anybody. And you would never have any reason to get upset again—ever!

When we dare to look fear in the eyes, we realize that we have nothing to fear, because we *are* innately good. And when we're not afraid to fail, we can't. "Success" is not in the result, but the effort. Doing what we know to do—right here, right now, the best we can do it—makes the consequences of doing it irrelevant. So, there is no failing! We don't have to wonder if we should have or could have done better. We can let go—not to give up on something, but to be at peace with everything. We are home free; nothing can hurt us. Let's say I'm afraid to get up and talk in front of a group—I don't want to make a fool of myself. Well, what if I know I'm not a fool? Then the worst thing that can happen is I'll *look* like a fool. Messing up doesn't change me . . . and neither does somebody else's perception of me change me. I can trust that I'm not a fool, and that I will learn from the experience. I can trust that experience is a good teacher and stand up and do my best. But what if I didn't prepare? I can't go back in time and prepare, but I can do my best right now. That's all I can ever do—my best right now—but it paves the way for doing better next time. I mustn't kid myself into thinking that I can bypass this time and still do better next time.

I can get up and do my best or I can let fear hold me back . . . in my seat, in a job I hate, or in a relationship that's unhealthy. To move forward, I have to venture out of my comfort zone. I have to face my fear—even if it seems insignificant, because fear is never insignificant. It is darkness. To face our fear is to choose good; it is to believe in our goodness. To ignore our fear or succumb to it is to choose evil. There is no evil without fear. *There is no darkness without fear, because without fear we trust the darkness, we light the darkness.* Without fear, we trust the unconscious.

"A problem cannot be solved at the same level of consciousness in which it was created," said Albert Einstein. And when we venture into the darkness, we venture into another level of consciousness. We venture into the truth of who we are, the power of who we are, the power of love. But we do not want to face what we fear is painful. We avoid it at almost any cost. Instead of meeting it head-on, we run the other way. We try to escape and meet with dead ends and addictions instead. We live in hiding, and often it seems we have to grapple with our darkness, much the way Jacob wrestled with the mysterious "stranger," only to find out with the dawn that he had actually wrestled with God all night. And henceforth, he would be called "Israel," translated "one who struggles with God" (you can read the story in Genesis, Chapter 32). When we are face-to-face with our darkness and the light shines, we might just find ourselves face-to-face with the best of who we are. "Face your deficiencies and acknowledge them; but do not let them master you. Let them teach you patience, sweetness, insight. When we do the best we can, we never know what miracle is wrought in our life, or in the life of another," said Helen Keller.

Karen Armstrong, the best-selling author of *The Spiral Staircase: My Climb Out of Darkness,* tells us how "Her deep solitude and a terrifying illness—diagnosed only years later as epilepsy—marked her forever as an outsider." She felt like a failure as a nun, as an academic, and as a normal woman capable of intimacy. Had she not *faced* that darkness, perhaps she would not have found the ecstasy and transcendence she failed to feel as a nun.

Maybe you have a terrible scar or a handicap or a disease. Maybe you were abused. Maybe you assaulted another human being. It is not the thing itself that is dark; it is your evaluation of it. In actuality, darkness is fear or a false belief. "If you are distressed by anything external, the pain is not due to the thing itself but to your own estimate of it; and this you have the power to revoke at any moment," said Marcus Aurelius, a Roman emperor and philosopher who lived two thousand years ago. The fight between the good wolf and the evil wolf does not define us, nor does it have to distress us. When we realize that it makes us human—and not evil—we can face the evil wolf, or the darkness, with hope.

Maybe your darkness seems hopeless—because it's yours. What if it were somebody else's, but not just anybody's—what if it were your child's? Could you forgive it? Could you shed light on it? Could you point out what was to be learned from it or how it made him special? Could you help him to face it and move on? Or would you reinforce the shame and help him bury it deeper? I ask these questions knowing that you may very well have treated a child's darkness the way you have treated your own. But would you do it again? Do you want to continue doing it?

Whatever the darkness, if you cling to it out of fear, you also cling to shame. And until you expose it to the light, it will fester. It will get uglier and uglier, more and more embarrassing—but not really. No matter how long it has been there and no matter how abominable it seems, light can shine on it. We know how it feels to venture into a dark room; we also know how it feels to find the light switch. When we have turned the light on, it is no longer dark. There is no darkness that light doesn't displace, no night that day doesn't follow. There is no fear that love doesn't overcome. Love is like light . . . it does not struggle to overcome fear anymore than light struggles to overcome darkness. Where light is, there is no darkness. Where love is, there is no fear. Love doesn't find it any more difficult to displace your fear than mine. The struggle is in finding the light, or the love, and aligning with it—mostly because we've buried it, and we're afraid to uncover it. We need only trust that what's there deep inside us is good.

"I suspect that it is by entering that deep place inside us where our secrets are kept that we come perhaps closer than we do anywhere else to the One that, whether we realize it or not, is of all our secrets the most telling and the most precious we have to tell," says Frederick Buechner.

We must come to realize that our darkness, or our struggle, is intended. We cannot recognize the light without the darkness. We cannot choose the light without the darkness. A lifetime may seem a long time to discern the difference between good and evil *and* choose good. But that is the goal of this lifetime—and every step, every stumble of the journey leads us toward that goal. We have no purpose except to love well. And to love well, we must come to know the truth—or the love—of who we are and choose to align with that truth. There *is* no other purpose! What else could we want to do?

Letting Go of False Beliefs

We have grown up with many myths. Some we are afraid to question and long for permission on "good" authority to let go of. Love gives us permission to explore invalid beliefs, release them, and replace them, because love is not afraid; it is not threatened. If we have a belief that doesn't serve our highest good, it is invalid. That means if you have a belief that limits you, it is invalid. If you have a belief that says you are unattractive, or stupid, or weak, it is invalid. If you have a belief that says you are inadequate or inferior, it is invalid. If you have a belief that indicates that you are something other than love, something other than good, it is invalid. Let go of that belief; replace it with a belief that serves you.

Your beliefs act as gatekeepers, letting things, people, and emotions in and out of your life. If there is something missing in your life, something you want, and you can't seem to get it, look at your beliefs to see which one is keeping what you want from you. And change it. Likewise, if there is something that detracts from your life, something you want to get rid of, look at your beliefs to see which one clings to it. And change that belief.

Your beliefs determine your behavior. Maybe you have a yearning to paint but learned that you were not artistic like your brother. Or maybe you learned that you couldn't earn a living as an artist, and that made it a frivolous endeavor. Maybe you learned something else that sounds equally stupid now, something that was never true to begin with. Any belief that stifles you is rooted in fear. It keeps you in the dark. It keeps the light out. It keeps love at bay.

Changing that belief is using rational emotive behavior therapy (REBT), a form of cognitive behavior therapy developed by Albert Ellis in 1955. REBT is an action-oriented psychotherapy that teaches individuals to examine their own thoughts, beliefs, and actions and replace those that are self-defeating with more life-enhancing alternatives. The fundamental premise of REBT is that people to a large degree disturb, upset, and defeat themselves through how they construct their view of reality by the means of their evaluations, beliefs, and philosophies about negative events in addition to the events themselves!

We can let go of beliefs—and myths—that don't serve us without betraying those who with good intentions passed them on. We can embrace the love. And we can forgive the fear, ours and theirs. We do not want to hold on to blame or guilt anymore than we want to hold on to lies.

It is in the light that we recognize false beliefs. It is in the light that we see the truth. We have to be willing to hit the light switch and deal with the uncertainty of what we will find. We have to *believe* that the truth is an ally, an advocate for us and for love. We have to believe that the only way to reap the benefits of the truth—whatever it is—and move forward is to turn the light on. The truth is not going anywhere. Ignoring it is not the answer. The longer we leave our fears in the dark, the more time we have to inflate the "evil" that awaits us. When we let go of false beliefs, we have nothing left to fear. And when we have nothing to fear, we have no reason to worry, get defensive, greedy, impatient, or angry. We have nothing to be ashamed of—nothing in our past and nothing in our future.

To reverence life, we must ask irreverent questions. We must look at the truth presented by anthropologists, psychologists, and theologians. But, ultimately, we must rely on God's truth as he has written it on our inward parts. Without the fear that clouds it, we can see it clearly. We can feel it. The truth sets us free of old, ill-founded beliefs. And when we have released the lies, we can establish new beliefs based on the truth. We can put our faith in love, our essence, everything good. *That's* what we are called to believe in. According to the Gospel of Luke, Jesus said, "If you had faith like a mustard seed, you would say to this mulberry tree, 'Be uprooted and be planted in the sea,' and it would obey you" (Luke 17:6).

We are afraid of lighting what's deep within us, not just because it may be evil, but because it may be magnificent. What if we put ourselves out there, believing that we are good, only to get shot down? What if we speak to the mulberry tree and it doesn't hear us? What if we're wrong? What if we fail? We're back to our worst nightmare. Ah, but what if we're right? What if the mulberry tree up and moves? Where do we go from there? That is, as they say, a tough act to follow. It might be more than we can live up to— more than we want to live up to. What might be required of us if we could move trees or mountains?

We must be willing to put ourselves out there to move beyond the fight or flight instinct, to be fully human . . . or to fully love, as the case may be. We must turn the light switch on and see what there is to see.

Happy and Free

It was not long after my encounter with the naked-man painting that I began to explore the depth of my pain. Oh, I had explored it all right, and I had even healed a great deal of it, but that only led the way for more healing. In October 1998, I quit my day job to write full-time. The last time I'd quit a job to start my own business—making angels accompanied by little verses— was in 1987, and I got scared and gave up too soon. I was not about to do that again. You see, I had just gone through a divorce—yes, a second divorce—and this time I had only stayed married for nine months. Initially, I was devastated; I couldn't believe I had been such an idiot. After fifteen years of being (at least on the surface) very happily single, I had finally gotten married again. How could I have possibly waited that long and still married the wrong one? But somewhere in there—before I moved from our big house into a condo—I began to feel very grateful for my life. It was as though I had almost lost it! Melodramatic, I know, but I realized that I liked *me*, and that I did not want to lose myself for my husband, or for anyone. Never had I felt so happy and free! I had faced my own darkness, hit the switch, and holy cow, holy Moses, holy Jan, I liked what I saw!

I was no longer—as far as I knew—afraid to fail, as a writer or anything else. My first surprise was that so many other people were afraid. I kept hearing almost exactly the same words over and over, "God, I wish I had the guts to do that." The guts to do what—to follow a dream, to quit a job that you're not passionate about, to try to earn a living doing something you've talked about for more than a decade, to try, to fail, to succeed . . . to learn the truth of what you're capable of? The alternative isn't pretty!

"The most challenging stranger is life itself, or the soul, the face and source of vitality. Life is always presenting new possibilities, and we may fear that bountifulness. It may seem safer to be content with what we have and what we are, and so we cling to the status quo. But in these matters there is no convenient plateau. When we refuse a new offering of life, we develop emotional calluses. The habit of acting from fear sets in quickly and becomes steadily more rigid. Refusing life, we become attendants of death," says Thomas Moore in his book *Original Self.*

We must choose between light and darkness, between good and evil, between love and fear, between our ego self and our true self.

Love Is the Funeral Pyre

Love is
The funeral pyre
Where I have laid my living body.

All the false notions of myself
That once caused fear, pain,

Have turned to ash
As I neared God.

What has risen
From the tangled web of thought and sinew

Now shines with jubilation
Through the eyes of angels

And screams from the guts of
Infinite existence
Itself.

Love is the funeral pyre
Where the heart must lay
Its body.

—Hafiz of Shiraz,
a fourteenth-century Sufi poet

CHAPTER FOURTEEN

Looking at Our Essence, Which Is Love, or Everything Good

WHOEVER POSSESSES GOD IN THEIR BEING,
HAS HIM IN A DIVINE MANNER, AND HE SHINES OUT
TO THEM IN ALL THINGS; FOR THEM ALL
THINGS TASTE OF GOD AND IN ALL THINGS
IT IS GOD'S IMAGE THAT THEY SEE.

—MEISTER ECKEHART

ANY NEGATIVE OR painful emotion that we have cries out from the ego and can be traced to fear, and any fear we have can be traced to the ultimate fear—the fear that something is innately wrong with us, the fear that we are somehow not quite good enough. When we light our darkness, or invalidate our ultimate fear, we invalidate all of our fears. Where there is no fear, there is perfect love—our essence!

Without fear, we see love in its purest form. Everything good that love is now has the stage. And we have front row seats! Nothing crosses our path that does not cry out love. We know what we have always known on some level—love is all there is! And at our core, that's what we are. Love. Our energy, our spirit, our essence—whatever label you want to use—is love. According to both the Christian and Jewish scriptures, the prophet Jeremiah said, "The Lord says 'I will put my law in their inward parts, and write it in their hearts'" (Jeremiah 31:33).

And Jesus sums up the law in virtually one word, "Love." An expert in the law tested him by asking, "Teacher, which is the greatest commandment in the Law?" Jesus replied, "'Love the Lord your God with all your heart and with all your soul and with all your mind,' this is the first and greatest commandment. And the second is like it, 'Love your neighbor as yourself.' All the Law and the Prophets hang on these two commandments" (Matthew 22:37–40).

There was no written New Testament scripture at the time, so Jesus was saying that everything in the scripture as they knew it hung on love. He was also saying that to love your neighbor as yourself was like loving God! *Everything* you need to know is found in love, everything about what's right, everything about ethical living, everything about God and your neighbor, peace and war, ritual and prayer, doctrine and leadership, success and valor is found in love. And that love is written on your inward parts. Somebody wrote *something* on our inward parts. "We could note the brain that is the body's apex; with its 10 billion neurons any one of which can be related to as many as 25,000 others for a number of possible associations that exceeds the number of atoms in the universe," wrote Huston Smith in *Forgotten Truth: The Common Vision of the World's Religions.*

It doesn't matter what religion, if any, you ascribe to; what matters is that you ascribe to love. That is, in fact, the filter that you must use to test any religious (or secular) belief—does it correspond with what you know love to be? Does it correspond with what is written on your heart? Does it resonate with what you innately know? Can you practice it and be in alignment with your essence?

The only obstacle between us and knowing—I mean really knowing—the love, the everything-good that's in our hearts, is fear! Once we grasp that, we are emboldened to let go of fear and to find the love we've buried beneath it. "A human being has so many skins inside, covering the depths of the heart. We know so many things, but we don't know ourselves! Why, thirty or forty skins or hides, as thick and hard as an ox's or bear's, cover the soul. Go into your own ground and learn to know yourself there," said Meister Eckehart.

It is in that ground that we unearth the proverbial pearl of great price that Jesus likened to the Kingdom of Heaven that we can trade everything else off for (Matthew 13: 45-46). *Love is all we need!* When we find it, we can stop dreaming of what could be and awaken to what is. We *are* love. *We are everything good, untainted by fear.* Evil has no hold on us; it is not our nature, it is only an alternative. Darkness, like falling down, is just a stage of learning. "Your vision will become clear only when you can look into your own heart. Who looks outside, dreams; who looks inside, awakens," said Carl Jung.

You always knew that you possessed strength that you hadn't really tapped into. You knew momentary bliss. There were times when you felt as though you could merge with the woods or sit and listen to the waves until the sun came up and went down again. And you've seen glimpses of your beauty. But there was always something haunting you, something calling you away from the peace, something demanding your attention. *That something* was always fear. Fear is the only obstacle that can keep you from the fullness of love, unbounded strength, unprecedented beauty, and unshakable peace and joy. There is no scarcity in love. There is no shortcoming in love. And there is no shortcoming in you.

Love Is Everything Good

I looked out at a gymnasium full of "at risk" young women participating in a Job Corps event and tried to make eye contact. Some of them seemed to deliberately ignore me; others seemed to deliberately stare, as if to say, "Yeah, come on, do you have anything worth listening to?" Mostly, they seemed more interested in each other than in me. Some of them had already birthed two or three children; some of them had found chastity and were pointing the proverbial finger at those who were "hanging out of their clothes." It was to this crowd that I posed the question, "What is love?" One of the young women in the front, as if she were recalling the words of a grandmother that suddenly took on new meaning, said "Love . . . is everything good." And when I said, "Yes!" I think they could hear enough conviction in my voice that they—at least some of them—decided to give me a chance.

Love *is* everything good! The Apostle Paul is credited with saying, "If I speak in the tongues of men and of angels, but have not love, I am only a resounding gong or a clanging cymbal. If I have the gift of prophecy and can fathom all mysteries and all knowledge, and if I have a faith that can move mountains, but have not love, I am nothing. If I give all I possess to the poor and surrender my body to the flames, but have not love, I gain nothing.

"Love is patient, love is kind. It does not envy, it does not boast, it is not proud. It is not rude, it is not self-seeking, it is not easily angered, it keeps no record of wrongs. Love does not delight in evil but rejoices with the truth. It always protects, always trusts, always hopes, always perseveres.

"Love never fails" (1 Corinthians 13:1–8, New International Version).

Are you painting a picture of love? If you still have trouble getting love on your canvas, try to paint everything good. Try to paint everything you want in your life. You cannot paint something good, you cannot *think* of something good that is not a part of love. Peace? It's in there. Joy? Got it! Friends? The world is full of them! Money? More than you need, until you start sharing it with all those friends, but then it multiplies! Sex? It's served with divine love! Everything you have ever wanted is yours.

And everything you have ever wanted to be—except afraid—
you are! Nothing and nobody can hurt you. You no longer have
issues to blame somebody else for or make excuses for. You no
longer have anybody to be jealous of—there's nobody you'd rather
be! Why be angry? What is there to resent? Your goodness is innate.
It is not contingent on anything or anybody. You don't care if
somebody else is "messed up," or if somebody doesn't recognize
how very important your time is, or if somebody lies to you.

You feel compassion and empathy for people who are in pain.
But you also feel respect for them. You know what they are made
of. You know they will find their way. Perhaps you will have the
privilege of helping them, but you will not help them with judgment or pity. You will help them by seeing their worth and helping *them* to see it. You will help them by demonstrating care,
based on what you know about them. That's the only way you
can help them. And you do that without demonstrating any con-
descension, because you don't feel any! You see the same essence
in others that you see in yourself. You *cannot* know your essence
without also knowing theirs.

You are no longer *striving* to be kind or loving, and you are not
trying to persuade somebody else that you are. You are not anxious about what they recognize in you or who they perceive you
to be. You are not trying to get your needs met through them.
You are not trying to control anything or everything. You are not
concerned about your reputation or your world crashing in on
you. Love cannot be squashed or diminished or altered in any
way. It is. You are. Without fear. There is nothing to stop you.

Maybe it's not clear yet exactly how fear gets in the way. Let me give you a personal example. I was in Morristown, New Jersey, where my column ran in the local newspaper, giving a talk. The last time I was there Robert from New York City (about an hour away) came to hear me. After tonight's talk he would whisk me back to his apartment in Manhattan and then see me off to the airport the next day, Saturday. While we talked that night over shrimp dumplings (the best I've ever had, delivered in minutes), I learned that he would attend an intimate charity event spearheaded by Deepak Chopra that Sunday. In my "dreams," I would ask if I could stay an extra night and attend the event with him. My new book *Naked Relationships* had just been published, and I would have liked nothing more than to put a copy right into the flesh-and-blood hand of Deepak Chopra, one of my heroes.

It was apparent that evening that Robert's arms and heart and mind were wide-open to me. We had a magical time, and he was already planning a trip to walk my stretch of the beach in Florida. Surely he would have welcomed me for another night of bliss, another shot at consummating bliss. What held me back? Only one thing—fear.

I could bask in the evening with Robert. Enchanting men was within the realm of what I could believe for. Leaving them wanting was right there in my comfort zone. Robert had called me in Florida after picking up one of my other books in the lobby of a friend's medical practice. He didn't just call me because he thought I was pretty; he called me because the book resonated with something inside of him. But I still had more confidence in my "pretty" and my kisses than I had in my ability to write a book that was worthy of Deepak Chopra's flesh-and-blood hand.

My publisher had already sent the book, or a galley, off to somebody on Deepak Chopra's staff. I had personally sent the book—maybe a few of them—off to Oprah's staff. But when faced with a real-life opportunity, I was scared. I caved. I didn't act in the power of love. I acted in the power of fear. Fear displaced my love, my *true* power.

This is not an exception to the rule. This is the rule. Fear displaces love, often without our knowing it. We are love, but fear, like evil, remains available to us. And one always overrides the other. We do not, we cannot, act from both. In any given moment, we act from one or the other. We choose—whether consciously or unconsciously. We cannot choose both at the same time; we *can* alternate between them and get mixed results. The opportunity was a result of my choosing love. The lost opportunity was a result of my choosing fear.

"The golden opportunity you are seeking is in yourself. It is not in your environment; it is not in luck or chance, or the help of others; it is in yourself alone," said O. S. Marden, the founder of *Success* magazine. It does not matter what Deepak Chopra would have done with my book. What matters is what *I* did with my book—a thing rooted in love or a thing rooted in fear. Love grows good fruit— abundance, faith, truth, peace. Fear grows doubt, self-consciousness, anxiety, and control. But those negative emotions are intended to teach us good lessons. They teach the lessons over and over and over again, until we are ready to learn them. That was five years ago.

When we sensitize our awareness of fear and then look at it when we feel it, we realize that we have nothing to fear. We realize that our fear is ill-founded. I was not ready for Deepak Chopra, but the reason I was not ready was fear. I *am* ready now, because I have looked at the darkness (or the hurt) that fear pointed to. I have shined a light on it. I did not have enough faith in myself or *Naked Relationships* to risk rejection from Deepak Chopra. I have more faith in the book now than I did then. But what if it was a lousy book—wouldn't I have benefited from learning that? Wouldn't I have benefited from finding out what was wrong with the book and how to write a better one? We do not have to be afraid of the truth! It is always our friend; it *cannot* lead us in the wrong direction. And feedback, no matter how painful at the time, is like falling down; it's a valuable part of learning. You don't have to worry about where it's coming from; use it for good, regardless.

Let me tell you another story that took place about two or three years later. Michael Guffy, a psychologist and dear friend, and I were facing each other on my favorite chaise. We talked of fear. And I shared with him a conscious fear that I still held. Are you ready for this? I was afraid to sing "Happy Birthday"! It started with my music teacher in middle school. One day as we all sang and she walked around the room, she stopped in close proximity to me. As she turned and walked away from me, I heard her muffled voice, "Monotone." That wasn't really the beginning, though; that brought to mind an earlier incident. That time my mom and sister and I sang at the kitchen table at the prompting of a family friend named Clyde. When we finished the song, my mom suggested that I sing "Sweet Jesus" with her. I knew deep down, *only* because of the expression on my mom's face, that I had not sung the first song well and that she was giving me a chance to redeem myself. And still earlier, I remember my mom explaining to people that the boys (she had four girls and two boys) developed an ear for music before the girls did. Ms. Prego, our music teacher, "Frog" as the middle school children called her, had confirmed my ineptness.

Later, in my twenties, I took singing lessons—right along with image and home-decorating seminars and tennis lessons. No weakness would be spared professional help. Only, my professional, loving, and very competent music teacher was unable to help me! So I just moved my lips at birthday parties when it was time to sing "Happy Birthday." And as part of a big birthday-celebrating family, I have done a lot of lip-synching.

So, there I sat with Michael, a we-can-say-anything friend and loving psychologist, and he quietly, knowingly asked, "Would you like to sing 'Happy Birthday' to me now?" I have, probably with some eloquence, just explained to Michael that I want *no fear* in my life and that I still had at least one ongoing fear of which I was aware. With unconditional love and acceptance, he asked if I'd like a chance to demonstrate that I didn't have to be afraid. I could not! As much as I wanted to, I could not sing "Happy Birthday" to Michael.

Two days later, I noticed a birthday marked on my calendar for Bob Leland. Bob is legally blind and lives in an efficiency apartment. I love Bob. I called his friend and neighbor Lance. "Hey, it's Bob's birthday—what should I get him?" With *no* hesitation, Lance said, "Oh, a cake! Bring a cake, knock on my door, and we'll walk over and sing 'Happy Birthday' to Bob." I had been given a second chance! I knew I had to take it. And I want you to know that when I sang "Happy Birthday" at Bob's door, I did it with all of my heart. My love for Bob on his birthday was enough to displace my fear. I had been given a second chance. And I had been given a perfect example of how love overrides fear when we let it. I'm not telling you how I sounded, because I don't know. It didn't matter. I was not trying to impress Bob; I was loving him. And I was singing from that pure place of love inside. That is our essence! Love. We can't find it until we displace fear.

You see, when I dreamed of placing my book in Deepak Chopra's hands, I was thinking of me and my book. I was even thinking of my own inadequacy, my *need* for help, and my getting that help from Deepak Chopra. I was not thinking of how much my book would help *other* people, though that's why I wrote it! I was not thinking of the power of love. It had somehow slipped my mind that love was my source—not Deepak! I was coming from fear; that's not our essence.

Love is boundless. It uses Deepak Chopra, but it doesn't need him anymore than it needs you or me. Eventually, it will have us, though. We are a part of love. Love is a part of us. We are part and parcel of the same essence. And that essence, that spirit, that force of love is our source. It is all the source we need—all the power, the strength, the faith, the wealth, the connection, the substance, the resilience, the sophistication, the good taste, the winsome charm, the confidence, the perseverance. Whatever you think you need, whatever good thing you want, you have in love! You just woke up and realized that you are the person you always wanted to be! Because you *are* love—it is more than your source; it's what you are!

When I have no fear, nothing can hold me back—there is nothing else that can hold love back. When I have no fear, nothing lures me off center. When I have no fear, there is nothing to separate me from love. But we are so accustomed to fear's sway that we take it for granted, unless we have sensitized ourselves to both love and fear. Then fear sounds a warning bell.

Maybe you sell real estate. A typical buyer might want to shop on weekends when you'd prefer to be with family. Maybe you steer them away from weekends by telling them that there's more freedom to look when people are at work during the week. Or maybe you cater to your buyers, wanting to do what's best for them—in spite of the fact that it's not best for you or your family. See how natural it *seems* to compromise your values? It's not about whether you work weekends or not; it's about whether you're loving or not. Love isn't afraid of losing the sale or offending the client or making a spouse angry. Love is honest and straightforward. It lets the chips fall where they may. It's not *really* natural or painless to compromise your values; it leaves you feeling off center and resentful. We struggle with good and evil because we need practice to recognize fear for what it is. We struggle to find peace of mind because it can only be found in love.

Maybe you feel unrest in your relationship and don't really know why. You are somehow deviating from love. Look at how and where and why. You might be afraid of losing him because your skin is losing resiliency and those little lines are getting deeper. You might resent her earning more money than you do. To know what's wrong or what's missing, all you have to do is look for negative emotion. It always points to fear, and behind the first fear of, say, wrinkles, is the ultimate fear of not being good enough.

If you're still not convinced that your negative emotion is rooted in fear, please look at another example of your negative emotion, *any* example. We have to get rid of the fear for you to truly see your essence of love. Maybe you feel a slight pang when your sister comes to visit. What is it about your relationship that's painful? Maybe she assaulted your decision to work when your son was young; maybe she questioned your choice of men. And maybe since then, you have felt intimidated or indignant. What she really did is trigger your insecurity about your decision to work or your choice in men. She triggered your fear that you messed up, that you were destined to mess up, that you didn't really have what it takes to be the kind of mother you wanted to be or get the kind of husband you wanted to have.

Maybe (I have a pretty good chance of being right on this one) your mother or father does something that grates on you. Maybe your dad always has to have the last word. It seems so obvious to you—you could record the conversations and hand them over for bad examples in a textbook. What most irritates you in your mother or father just might be a trait you share with them, a trait you have despised in yourself and disowned, a trait that threatens your ego, or the image you have of yourself.

When I counsel people in my home, I like to have fresh flowers in the room. A client who was to have a session by phone one morning called and asked if it was okay to come by instead. He was in a neighboring city and wanted to drive over. I said, "Sure." Later, I realized that the fresh flowers on the table downstairs were all but dead. I made a quick trip to the neighborhood florist—or I tried to make a quick trip—and somebody immediately pulled in front of me. I said, "Oh, shit!" Under normal circumstances, I could have had the fresh flowers in the water and on the table in twelve and a half minutes. I didn't have fifteen minutes. But, "Oh, shit!" is a reliable sign of negative emotion. I had to look—knowing what I would find—at what was going on for me. Flowers on the table aren't critical, but I had linked them to my professionalism and my ability to help somebody. Being back before the coaching client arrived was not critical, either, but I had also linked that to my professionalism and ability to help somebody.

Fresh flowers do help me to feel centered. The guy who pulled up in the big truck, though, probably didn't care too much about the flowers. He was much more interested in learning how to fix the relationship he had "screwed up." Being punctual is responsible and considerate, but "shit" happens. And when it does, it does not make us irresponsible, inconsiderate, unprofessional, or *bad*. Our awareness of "shit" and our ability to choose it or love is what makes us human. It's what I do with the stuff that defines me. In fact, what I do with the stuff defines it as well. I don't have to see it as "shit." I can see it as an opportunity for learning and growth.

We *are* love. When we trust that we are love, we can stop obsessing about our "imperfections" (and everybody else's) and recognize their role in leading us to perfection—and let them. I don't have to be perfect to be love. But I have to be willing to look at what doesn't feel perfect to me. I have to be willing to look at what I'm afraid of. And when I do, I will always learn that I have nothing to fear. My ultimate fear is invalid. I have no fear that is not rooted in the fear of falling short or not being good enough, not measuring up, failure, however you want to word it. Please don't let semantics get in your way. If you do not face the pain, you cannot heal it. If you do face it, you will surely heal it. You are innately good, innately love.

When we realize that we have nothing to be afraid of, we stop allowing fear in all its many forms—anger, impatience, greed, ego, deception, scarcity, blame, defensiveness, jealousy, anxiety, worry, hatred, resentment, bitterness—to drive us. We stop allowing our egos to drive us. Fear, no matter what form it takes, displaces love. There is only love and fear, or good and evil. And fear, or evil, is invalid. Please stay with me. "Good is positive. Evil is merely privative, not absolute: it is like cold, which is the privation of heat. All evil is so much death or nonentity," said Ralph Waldo Emerson. As long as we feed the good wolf, the evil wolf is a nonentity! *Fear exists only in the absence of love.*

And we are love. We were never really separate. We were just afraid.

Part Four

Being Who We Are ...
It Means Overcoming
Our Separateness

CONTINUE UNTIL YOU SEE
YOURSELF IN THE CRUELEST PERSON
ON EARTH, IN THE CHILD STARVING,
IN THE POLITICAL PRISONER. PRACTICE
UNTIL YOU RECOGNIZE YOURSELF IN
EVERYONE IN THE SUPERMARKET,
ON THE STREET CORNER, IN A

CONCENTRATION CAMP,
ON A LEAF, IN A DEWDROP.
MEDITATE UNTIL YOU SEE YOURSELF
IN A SPECK OF DUST IN A DISTANT
GALAXY. SEE AND LISTEN WITH
THE WHOLE OF YOUR BEING.
IF YOU ARE FULLY PRESENT,
THE RAIN OF DHARMA WILL WATER
THE DEEPEST SEEDS IN YOUR STORE
CONSCIOUSNESS, AND TOMORROW,
WHILE YOU ARE WASHING THE
DISHES OR LOOKING AT THE BLUE SKY,
THAT SEED WILL SPRING FORTH,
AND LOVE AND UNDERSTANDING WILL
APPEAR AS A BEAUTIFUL FLOWER.

—THICH NHAT HANH

EVEN AFTER WE *know* who we are, *being* who we are takes practice.

Love is everything good; it is the force that connects us; it is our essence; it is our God. It is a science; it is an art. We must learn it, cultivate it, practice it, and *be* it. Doing so is the journey of a lifetime, a journey we are innately prepared to take.

Taking the journey means shedding our egos and, thus, overcoming our separateness. Taking the journey—not reaching a preconceived state or destination—means reclaiming the tranquility of "paradise" with an awareness of both our oneness and our sovereign choice. It means knocking on the door of Nirvana or Enlightenment; it means entering the Kingdom of Heaven. That kingdom is within. It is the pearl of great price, the treasure that is enduring and unfailing, the treasure that cannot be destroyed or altered or torn from us. Love.

Three Steps to *Being* Love

- Invoke love—sit quietly and find the love within and the love without that resonates with it; commune with love to understand love's nature, your nature.

- Align with love—follow love's lead; consciously practice doing what love does.

- *Be* love—merge with love—body, mind, and spirit—to know oneness with love, to be all that love is, to be all that you are, untainted by fear.

CHAPTER FIFTEEN

Invoking Love

BE STILL AND KNOW THAT I AM GOD.

—KING DAVID, THE PSALMIST

IT IS IN our stillness that we know who God is. We cannot sense God or get to know his nature—or our nature—while we are engaged in our ego's doings. Just as we must sit quietly and give our attention to God to know him (or anybody else), we must sit quietly with love to know love. God is love. And it is in our stillness that we make time and space for love. It is in our stillness that we learn to transcend time and space—and ego.

In one of the villages Jesus entered, he was received into the home of a woman named Martha. And while he was there, Martha's sister Mary sat at Jesus's feet to hear his words. Martha, being burdened with serving, went to Jesus, the way a child might go to a parent, and asked, "Don't you care that my sister has left me alone to serve? Bid her to help me." But Jesus said, "Martha,

Martha, you are careful and troubled about many things. But one thing is needful; and Mary hath chosen that good part" (Luke 10:38–42).

Martha was like we are when we're too preoccupied with our egos to be present with love. She was like we are when we resent the burden we take on—as though somebody else bundled it up and placed it on our shoulders and we have no way out from under it. Surely that must be a time to seek divine intervention, right? Jesus didn't think so. But Martha's openness in approaching Jesus helped her to see the truth. When Jesus said that only one thing was needful, that didn't leave much room for Mary to wonder: "Well, doesn't somebody have to prepare food for you and your disciples?" or "You *will* need some fresh water, won't you?" It's amazing how we can fuss with a garnish on the dessert plate or fingertip towels in the guest bathroom, but forget to look our guests in the eye and connect with them while they are with us.

The most important aspect of invoking love is stillness, but that just might be our toughest challenge. And our *busyness* is often about fear: we're afraid of what others will think. We really do want to make a nice impression. And we'd feel guilty about just sitting there—like some people (Mary!) we know. Only one thing is needful, and that is to sit quietly at the proverbial feet of the teacher. We cannot truly reach out and invoke love, nor recognize it when it shows up, while we are distracted by the concerns of our egos. So anything that helps us to quiet the ego's chatter can become a channel for love. Prayer, meditation, other spiritual rituals, nature, and the arts—painting, poetry, dancing, music—are all conduits.

The aim of God in creation is communion. He wants to connect with us—not our egos. "The aim of art is to represent not the outward appearance of things, but their inward significance," said Aristotle. God created us to manifest our inward significance, his inward significance, his spirit, his love, and only by doing so can we connect and commune with him. By helping us to see more deeply than we can see with our eyes, conduits lead us into communion with love. The flickering flame of a candle can help us forget time and space. A flower or a handful of weeds from a child can help us transcend our busyness and clutter and touch the face of love. And when a poem, or a dance, or a piece of music, or art makes us close our eyes and go within, we are invoking love. . . . "Yes, please be with me." It is in that stillness, that openness, that we can connect and commune with love. No wonder man has a history of bringing nature and the arts into his attempts to connect with God.

Prayer and meditation, depending on the type you practice, can be very similar. I like to use meditation to quiet my mind and relax my body. Then I can be present for conversation and communion with God. Meditation generally involves being still with an awareness of your breath. When you focus on the relaxing rhythm of breathing, you are less distracted (dinner's at 7:00; I could be doing laundry). And meditation has been scientifically documented to produce physical signs of deep relaxation in heart rate, blood pressure, respiration, brain waves, and plasma cortisol (a hormone associated with stress). If you make meditation part of your lifestyle, you're likely to be less distracted, more present and calm, and generally refreshed. I do what I call my DP (for Daily Perspective) first thing each morning, before the clutter of everyday life has a chance to move in. I started it about twenty years ago when I realized that it was easy for me to lose the perspective I wanted to have through the course of the day. Over the years, it has evolved based on my understanding, but it still serves the same purpose. It helps me to quiet my mind, connect with God, and feel ready to meet the practical matters of my day with a spiritual—or loving—perspective. It helps me to start my day feeling centered, and to return to that center more readily if I get distracted. For me, this is where nature and the arts come in— when I find *them*, I find center.

We get stuck, though, when we anxiously look around (out of fear) and try to duplicate somebody else's way of invoking love. Then we go through the motions. You can look around to see what everybody else is doing. You can follow suit, kneel down, do some hand gestures, breathe, stretch, wave your arms in the air, chant, or sing—without feeling anything. You can read the books and spend thousands of dollars on workshops without getting it emotionally. Do what works for *you*, without complicating it. I think we find love within first (whether we realize it or not), so we know what it is we beckon. But when we feel it in the ocean, or a poem, or a ritual, it is because what is inside resonates with what is outside. As within, so without . . . and this we learn to consciously invoke.

We need not race about to try everything. You've seen people move from one thing to the next to the next, wondering, "Is this it?" We can become frustrated moving from piano lessons, to yoga classes, to Reiki sessions, to astrology, if we are searching for some elusive feeling or state. We can try everything, not wanting to miss out, and end up not truly "getting" anything. The idea is not to keep trying until lightning strikes us with love. The idea is to be tuned in to the love within, so that the love that's already all around us can resonate with what's inside. The love inside is the same as the love that's outside. Love is love wherever it is. And it is everywhere.

We don't *need* any structured prayer or ritual to invoke love or recognize love. Only one thing is needful—stillness, or an attentive, open heart. And we need not spend years seeking or asking questions *before* we sit with love. A very intelligent young woman in a roomful of people at Omega Institute raised her hand to ask me a question. She struggled with a nuance of how to love *everybody*. I had the sense that she didn't *really* want an answer. She wanted to continue seeking. If she were to get all the answers, she would have to start using them, but as long as she was still searching, she could postpone truly living and loving. And she seemed very adept at asking questions and eluding the answers.

When our intention is to invoke love—and not to put it off until we are ready for it—love shows up. Well, not exactly. Love is always there. It is felt, because we are open to it. And when we are expectant, our senses are heightened. We feel love, and we don't let the feeling flutter by. We stop and feel what we are feeling. Like a bird dog that picks up a scent, we stay with the feeling, we home in on it. We identify what triggers it, what intensifies it, and what stifles it or blocks it. And we act, we live, accordingly.

Just the other morning while my husband Sam and I were driving back from the beach to the farm, we spotted a black bear on the edge of the forest. I had never seen a bear in the wild and I squealed, "Sweetie, turn around, please turn around!" And then fumbling with the sunroof controls, while trying to stand up, I said, "Please get this open!" I had my head out of the roof in no time (without any further assistance), wanting to get as close as I could to the bear. Sam refused to let me out of the car, even before I had a chance to ask—what, am I a child? Well, sort of; and Sam is, among other things, a veterinarian. We would sit there—Sam would sit there, I would stand there on my seat with my head and half my body out the roof—for thirty minutes or more. I was in heaven. Other cars and trucks would come and go; some would take pictures. The bear indulged us. And I delighted in pointing out the bear to oncoming traffic—hey, they clearly wanted to know what was happening!

Before we drove off, Sam would consent to my getting out of the car. I was within twelve feet of the bear. I could see him stretch his head and his neck, his loose bear skin rippling as he did. I could see the light camel color around his black nose and the softness of his fur and his steps. I could see why somebody came up with teddy bears. This bear was snuggly and precious. And watching him helped me to feel connected with life, with love, with the forest behind him, with the earth, and with God. I was so pleased that we did not drive off sooner, that we did not leave when the bear temporarily retreated into the trees now and then. We stayed with him. We stayed with the feeling, the magic, the connection. There was no better way to spend our time. We were still hungry when we got to the blueberry pancakes, and we have never made such delicious blueberry pancakes as we did that morning.

If I realize that I am a vessel for love and I want love to flow through me, I am continually open to the love I encounter. I walk out the door to go for a jog, and a bird flies from the tree. Something inside of me is sparked; that something is love. I don't take the bird and the tree for granted and look at my watch as I hurry on. I have invoked love; and it has shown up! I look at the bird and befriend it; he is not just a bird. *He* is a pileated woodpecker. And the tree is a magnolia tree whose flowers are showing off large red seeds that dangle on little threads this time of year. There is a nest in the tree—maybe it is an old nest or maybe . . . I am saying good morning to the bird now and asking about the nest. I have identified a means of receiving the love that I have invoked. I am feeding the spark. I am letting love fill me and flow through me.

I will be able to feel love for the rest of the day. And I know how to reconnect when I'm challenged by fear. I know how to stay connected tomorrow and the next day. I park my desk in front of a window, jog, walk in the woods, feed the horses, stop for bears. And sometimes I get off center or disconnected—I know when it happens because I no longer feel free. I feel pushed or pulled—like there is not enough of me to go around, like I don't have enough time, or control, or power, or *something*. There is an anxious tugging that blocks the flow of love. That is when I must recognize that fear has slipped in—I *do* have enough of whatever I need. Love is enough. This is the time to stop and invoke love again. Love hasn't gone anywhere, but I have—not far, though—and the sooner I get back on track, the less squirming I do. I can sit still and breathe deeply, or ring my tingsha chimes, maybe smell a rose on my desk, go for a walk, or simply close my eyes and go within where the love is, so I can reconnect.

Staying Connected with Love

"No man ever followed his genius 'til it misled him," said Henry David Thoreau.

Our genius is love! As you go about your day, notice what resonates with the love inside of you. Keep in mind that love is what enlivens the best in you and in others. Perhaps there is a painting in the office, or a baby cow on the way to the office, or an old man in the elevator, or a piece of music on the radio. When love presents itself, be present with it. Follow it, or take it with you.

Don't wait for that song to play on the radio again. And don't buy a CD and listen to twelve other songs every time you want to tune in to love. Put that one song where you can access it with a button anytime you feel like it. And push the button over and over and over. Learn the song. Sing the song. Feel the song. Share the song. Live the song.

If it's a poem that connects your heart with heaven, make the poem part of your prayer and meditation. Print it and put it in your appointment book or on your refrigerator or your computer screen. Sit with the poem. Sleep with it under your pillow. Write your own poem. Write your own book of poems. Share it with the world—not just the poem, but the feeling, the connection, the love.

If it's a piece of art that makes you cry or sigh or gaze into love, feel the art. Sit with the color and the paint and the emotion. Feel what the artist felt. Become the artist and pour your being onto a canvas—the deepest part of you is what will resonate with the deepest part of somebody else. That's the part you have in common. Don't concern yourself with what it looks like or how "good" you are. You're good! Remember?

Artist Howard Ikemoto once shared, "When my daughter was about seven years old, she asked me one day what I did at work. I told her I worked at the college—that my job was to teach people how to draw. She stared at me, incredulous, and said, 'You mean they forget?'" He says that children draw unself-consciously, while adults frequently lose their ability to create without fear of judgment. When he was teaching, the first thing he told his beginning students was that they had to give themselves permission to draw, and that the rest would come very naturally. Don't forget that you can draw, or paint, or sing, or dance. A few lines from Joshua Kadison's "Painted Desert Serenade," a song that taps a bit of music deep inside my heart, say:

He tells her, I want to paint you naked on a big brass bed with bright orange poppies all around your head.

And she says, Crazy old man, I'm not young anymore.
That's all right, he whispers, I've never painted before.

Keep a charcoal pencil, box of markers, or an easel standing ready. Keep a fragrant flower on your night table. Keep a gong in your garden or chocolate truffles on your desk, and eat them with your eyes closed! Do what it takes to breathe in God, to get centered and feel present with love, with *you*. And as long as you connect with love, everything else will be okay—not because everything is transformed, but because your perception of it is transformed. I bring fresh flowers in from the field, or the woods, or the garden because they help me to stay connected. They don't zap everything that could interfere with my peace—they don't have to. They remind me to stop, to inhale them, to be present with them. And as long as I'm connected, there is nothing that can interfere with my peace. The flowers are a conduit for love.

Love is—everywhere and always—but it does not yell and scream for our attention. It waits until we make room for it, until we are willing to spend quality time with it. We cannot be led by fear into busyness and expect to meet love there. When we feel love resonate within us, it is because we are present with ourselves. We are not regretting the past or feeling anxious about the future. We are not drowning out the still, small voice. That doesn't mean you can't scream and dance with love. You can, but you don't have to. And you don't have to do the same thing all the time. You can be bold or tender, playful or serious, ringing with joy or quiet with peace.

But, you must quiet the ego's chatter to invoke love. Only then can you be sensitive to love's presence to commune with it. And we must commune with love and get to know love if we are to align with it.

CHAPTER SIXTEEN

Aligning with Love

A MUSICIAN MUST MAKE MUSIC,
AN ARTIST MUST PAINT, A POET MUST WRITE,
IF HE IS TO BE ULTIMATELY AT PEACE WITH HIMSELF.
WHAT A MAN CAN BE, HE MUST BE.

—ABRAHAM MASLOW

LOVE IS WHAT you can be. It is—if you are to reach peace—
what you *must* be. But to truly "be" love, first you must come
into alignment with love and consciously practice doing what
love does.

When you come face-to-face with your essence in communion
with love, you bask in it, you revel in it, but you don't, you can't,
keep it to yourself. You feel the music inside, and you know that
to manifest the love, you must move to the music. And you begin
to align with your music, with love. You start practicing with a
conscious awareness of what you are doing. Sometimes you mess

up. But you keep practicing until you have what we could call conscious competence. Along the way, you know moments of unconscious competence, moments when you are, effortlessly, better than you've ever been on any dance floor. You and the music are one! You and love are one!

Once we truly know who we are, we also know what love is. Aligning with who we are is aligning with love. It will take practice, but doing it is no longer in question. We must. And it feels way too natural, way too wonderful, to care what the outcome is. Loving really is its own reward. "What will you give me if I love you with my whole heart. . . . Never mind, I was going to do it anyway," says Brian Andreas, through one of his "story people."

As you'll recall from Chapter 12 (and your life, if you think about it), the only way to be happy is to be true to yourself. When we align with love, we align with our music, our essence, our values, our universe, our higher selves, our divinity, our God—call it what you will—and we have self-verification or self-esteem. We have happiness! We have what we need to move on to what psychologist Abraham Maslow called "self-actualization needs"—unity, balance, harmony, completion, justice, richness, simplicity, aliveness, beauty, benevolence, individuality, ease, truth, self-sufficiency, and meaningfulness. And life is as good as it gets . . . until it gets better . . . and from now on, it always gets better. It *only* gets better.

Whether you're ordering dinner or deciding where to live, with practice, you will discern what feels loving. One thing on the menu will be what your body needs, what feels good, what feels like "you." One place will feel like home, even if it's a new home; the other won't. Taking one job will be motivated by greed; taking the other will require trust. Greed is rooted in fear. Trust is rooted in love. One path will feel like growth; one will feel like escape. Love is growth, and it doesn't run away. When you're not sure what to do, just let love displace fear. Let truth displace lies. Let go instead of clinging. Trust instead of doubt. Forgive yourself instead of feeling guilty. Accept responsibility instead of being defensive or assigning blame to somebody else. See what you have in common rather than focusing on the differences. Stay present rather than regretting the past or fretting about the future. Choose happiness over self-pity, ego, anger, greed, or control. And play big—choose as though you cannot fail. You can't, because love can't.

It sounds simple. Try to keep it that way. Don't lose touch with what you feel by overanalyzing. Look for what's called "flow" in the science of positive psychology—it happens when you have no anxiety or fear of failure, allowing you to be highly productive and joyful with no sense of time. When you find yourself rationalizing or justifying, let that be a red flag. Trust your instincts. Trust yourself. Trust love. It won't let you down.

Manifesting Love

We are love, but it is only in aligning with love that we *manifest* who we are. The movie *Pan's Labyrinth* demonstrates this beautifully. Ofelia, a dreamy little girl with a remarkable combination of innocence and maturity, is still clinging to her fairy tales as she travels with her mother to meet her new stepfather. As commander of the rural military outpost that Ofelia is forced to make her new home, the captain is more interested in his son, carried by his expectant wife, than either his wife or Ofelia. Understandably, Ofelia withdraws more deeply into her fairy tales, taking us with her. She believes that her *real* parents were from a higher place, and that they still look for her return. She cannot be shown the way back to them, though, until she has demonstrated her own divine nature. Once she has aligned with her essence—provoked by a series of very tough choices—she is identified as the lost princess. And she returns to "paradise" with an awareness of her royalty *and* her choice to align with it!

By cultivating an awareness of our ongoing choice to love—rather than fear—we learn to align more closely with love, or the "music" of love. We manifest love; we share love. We show people what love looks like; we touch them with love, so they know how it feels. We cannot do otherwise. When we are aligned with love, we are also aligned with them, with their essence. We don't just grow into our oneness with love; we grow into our oneness with them, with life.

We know them, and we understand them. And when we understand people, we relate to them, we accept them. We love them. Think about it—have you ever gotten close enough to really know somebody and been disgusted by him? It is easy to judge somebody harshly from a distance. But love does not let you keep people at a distance. It gets you close enough to see their hopes and fears, their obstacles, their parents and their babies, their pain. People are lovable. And people have a context. It's when we take them out of context that we're apt to stand in judgment or hold up a scorecard or a guilty verdict.

As it turns out, the exercise of learning to choose good over evil—learning to recognize love, believe in it, and choose it, sometimes by faith—is the prerequisite to loving well. (Yes, it was part of God's plan.) When we tried to love others before we connected to the love within, we couldn't truly love them, because we were motivated by fear. We cared for them because we wanted somebody to care for us. We responded to their needs because we'd feel guilty if we didn't. We sought to please them because we couldn't please ourselves, and we desperately needed approval. We can love others only as well as we love ourselves. Love is an attitude of the heart. We love everybody—or nobody. And our biggest challenge in life is to love ourselves!

We cannot love well—ourselves or others—without knowing what love is, without knowing who we are. Love is always guided by knowledge. We cannot love God without knowing who he is. And he is love. As we choose love, we draw on love's strength to align with it. And when we embody love, we are also nurtured by it. We are empowered to continually recognize and choose love.

What, Exactly, Does Manifesting Love Look Like?

Let's spell love out, so that we can more consciously practice it, align with it, and get good at it. If you were to make a list of what "love is" and what "fear is," the lists might look something like this:

Love is:

Peace
Joy
Hope
Faith
Contentment
Harmony
Enough
Abundance
Beauty
Truth
Liberated
Equality
Generosity
Kindness
Benevolence
Compassion

Empathy
Letting go
Happiness
Alive
Enlivening
Unconditional
   acceptance
Enduring
Patient
Persevering
Resilient
Willing to start
   again
Forgiveness
Sincere
Genuine

Naked
Trusting
Intuitive
Responsible
Accountable
Orderly
Respectful
Present
Caring
Guided by
   knowledge
Unthreatened
Unity
Healthy
Free

Fear is:

Afraid
Anxious
Greed
Deceptive
Jealous
Irresponsible
Blame
Defensiveness
Anger
Hatred
Resentment
Doubt
Divisive
Narrow-minded
Threatened

Worried
Chaotic
Confused
Inequality
Inferiority
Superiority
Arrogant
Pretentious
Secretive
Scarcity
Disjointed
Skeptical
Regret
Self-pity
Guilt

Lies
Pride
Ego
Control
Judgment
Clinging
Bitterness
Misery
Justification
Self-consciousness
Insecurity
Depression
Unhealthy
Distracted
Stifled

You may find the lists repetitious, but you may also find them lacking. You can make your own lists. These are only intended to help you make a ready distinction between love and fear. Every time you feel uneasy, offended, distracted, or negative in any way, you have an opportunity to let go of fear, even if it's just the remnant of a fear you used to have. You might find yourself responding out of habit, a habit based on a fear you no longer have. Your awareness of what you're feeling will become increasingly heightened, and as a negative emotion rears its head, you can recognize it immediately as fear. You can trace it almost as quickly to the ultimate fear of not being good enough. And then you can, once again, invalidate it.

Knowing No Fear, We Know the Fullness of Love

"If you knew who walks beside you on this way which you have chosen, fear would be impossible," says *A Course in Miracles*. And with love, fear *is* impossible.

Without fear, we know all the *truth* of love. We are not afraid to look beneath the surface—there is no longer a mask, a basement, or a dark closet. There is no deception, no feigned improvements.

Without fear, we know all the *power* of love. There is no ceiling imposed by fear that prevents us from seeing the heavens or touching the heavens.

Without fear, we know the *peace* of love. And it can no longer be shaken.

Without fear, we know the *joy* of love. It is not contingent on a job, a church, or a spouse.

Without fear, we know the *hope* of love. It does not give up on what is good. It always believes.

Without fear, we know the *faith* of love. Love perseveres in the face of the impossible. It is the source of miracles.

Without fear, we know the *compassion* of love. Love is always caring, and it responds to need with respect. It does not offer a handout when it can offer a chance to contribute. Love sees the value of what people have to give, and the value of an opportunity to give it.

Without fear, we know the *abundance* of love. We want nothing in return for love. There is nothing we lack. We love because love is all there is.

Without fear, we know the *responsibility* of love. We do not blame somebody else for what only we can change. We are no longer at the mercy of somebody—anybody—else. Instead of feeling guilty for what we are not doing, we do what we want to be done.

Without fear, we know the *forgiveness* of love. We know we have learned from our "mistakes" enough to do better. We know the goodness of our humanity—and everybody else's.

Without fear, we know the *freedom* of love. We are liberated from striving to do anything we do not truly want to do.

Without fear, we know we cannot fail, because love *cannot fail.* We can love, we can live, as though we cannot be hurt. Because we can't.

With love, we know only learning to love better, learning to love more consistently, learning to get back on track more quickly, more easily.

When we align with love, we feed the "good wolf." Eventually, we do so without having to think about it too much or talk ourselves into it. We don't measure our words for fear that they betray our facade; we have no facade. We quit trying so hard. It is the striving that is exhausting. Doing is exhilarating—it does not drain us the way trying does. But our goal is one step beyond doing. Our goal is being (and we're saving that for the last chapter).

As we continue to align with love, we affirm over and over again that we are, indeed, good enough. And we watch the walls between us melt away as we move toward oneness. I may not know how many children you have or where you went to high school, but I know that at a core level you are love. I know that you face the same choices that I do. And I know that at any given moment you are doing the best you are able to do. I know that you have felt the pain of learning the hard way to choose love, just as I have. I know that if you could have done better in that moment, you would have, just the way I would have. And as we continue to align with love, we align with ourselves. We know self-verification or self-esteem. We know true happiness. And we cannot lose it—unless we deviate from love. Aah, but we will not stray from love; we have cultivated our awareness of love. We have cultivated our awareness of fear; we have unmasked it. Fear cannot slip in without our realizing it. Any negative emotion is really fear masquerading, and we know what the ultimate fear is. It is invalid.

When we feel negative emotion, we will not think, "Oh, I really am bad" or "You really are bad." We will think, "Oh, fear slipped in . . . it is invalid, and I will show it out." We will exercise choice. We will align with love. And somewhere along the way, perhaps while we're "washing the dishes or looking at the blue sky," we will flower into love, into *being* love.

CHAPTER SEVENTEEN

Being Love—
Innately More Than
We Ever Dreamed of Being

THE SEED OF GOD IS IN US.
GIVEN AN INTELLIGENT AND HARD-WORKING
FARMER, IT WILL THRIVE AND GROW UP TO GOD,
WHOSE SEED IT IS; AND ACCORDINGLY ITS FRUITS
WILL BE GOD-NATURE. PEAR SEEDS GROW
INTO PEAR TREES, NUT SEEDS INTO NUT TREES,
AND GOD-SEED INTO GOD.

—MEISTER ECKEHART

LOVE IS OUR God-seed. And just the way there is enough of whatever is needed in a little pear seed to grow into a pear tree, there is enough love in us to grow into God. And I have to believe that "God" is innately more than we ever dreamed of being. In love, there is enough of everything good, for whatever you could possibly have in mind. It is innate. It is inside of you. It *is* you.

And it is your knowledge of good and evil that allows you to demonstrate who you are. It is your choosing that allows you to learn the value of everything good, as well as the destruction of fear. It is your demonstration of who you are that gives legs to love, hands, and feet, and a voice to love. It is your growing up to be God that allows you to bear the fruit of God and propagate his love.

We can see glimpses of love, we can feel love, we can even exercise love without really knowing love. We are living the truth of who we are when we have shed the ego self and reconciled our true self, or our essence of love, with God. Then we know love, we know God, in the biblical sense. We share a mind and body, as well as a spirit, or seed. In neurotheology, findings suggest that mystical experiences, such as finding oneness with God, are actually accompanied by evidence in the brain that we're losing boundaries between ourselves and the external world.

By overcoming our separateness, we know the power of love. It is the same power, the same love that we have always known. But it is no longer limited by our ego self or our fear. We feel the true power of love, the true power of God. We no longer want to play small. We know how "big" we are. And the power is no longer latent. It is no longer sporadic.

Love doesn't just come out on special occasions or for special people. While Christmas is a fine day to get into the spirit, so is every other day. "Write in your heart that every day is the best day of the year," said Ralph Waldo Emerson. My husband and I have what we call a celebration tree—it is really a "Christmas tree" with little white lights on it, but it stays plugged in all year. As my friend Ben Campen likes to say, "Every day's a holiday; every meal's a banquet." And he means it. The man has the same gleam in his eye whether he's eating tuna fish out of a can or dining in an exquisite restaurant. And his love doesn't just come out for those special few that are easy to love. He adores his children and his grandchildren, but *nobody* leaves his presence without feeling his joy. "A person, who is nice to you, but rude to a waiter, is not a nice person. (This is very important. Pay attention. It never fails.)," says Dave Barry in his *16 Things That Took Me Over 50 Years to Learn*. And a person who loves you but not everybody else, doesn't really love you.

When we are living the truth of love, we have answered yes to the question, "Do you want to be happy?" And we have left off all the qualifiers. There is no, "Well, yes, but *of course* I'll be sad if I get cancer." Or, "*Nobody* can be happy if their spouse dies." Or, "Understandably, I'm upset when somebody wrongs me." We want to be happy no matter what. And we are! When I do one-on-one consultations, sometimes people have a whole litany of reasons—excuses, if you will—for why they don't or can't have a satisfying life. And after I have patiently listened as they aired all of their grievances, I ask, "Do you want to be happy anyway?" Some people think they are supposed to be sad or miserable until things change, but things aren't going to change so much that we can't find reasons to be unhappy—if we want to be unhappy.

And some people think that God is supposed to be sad when a child dies or an earthquake quakes. Or maybe they think God is oblivious, or maybe they want to know where he is while all of this is going on. God is. And he's always in the same place. Everywhere. I believe *God* sees himself in that "speck of dust in a distant galaxy." And I believe that God in all places is *always* happy. Do you imagine that the God who created the universe for his pleasure decides to take his marbles and go home or sulk? I don't want to lose you here, but what would happen if we all lived forever? What would happen if we had no disasters calling us together? What would happen if we had no occasion to learn the value of choosing love or the consequences of choosing evil? What would happen if we didn't learn to be responsible or accountable? I don't think God grieves when his plan is working. And I don't think he made a mistake and put the wrong plan into action. Do you?

When I am not afraid of my own cancer, or my own spouse's death, or my own disaster, then I am not afraid for you either. I don't want to disparage the magnificence of our physical bodies, or the planet, but they are not set up to last forever. They are set up for teaching us to love well. I was living in a three-story townhouse across from the Atlantic Ocean. Between me and the ocean was a two-lane road (that I conveniently washed from my view). It was the hurricane season of 2004—especially, it seemed, in Florida—and there was a mandatory evacuation. Only I was still there. I was doing a workshop in Martha's Vineyard during the first evacuation that year, and I decided to stay home for this one.

But before the hurricane struck, I walked over to the ocean and befriended it. I did not want to rise up against the hurricane— come on, I am a reasonable girl. I wanted to show my respects; I wanted to appreciate the magnitude of what was coming and join with it. Why make it an enemy? The winds hurled the water as far as I could see. There were no waves crashing to the shore with a calm sea against the horizon. It was all one ongoing rage. I stood there like a little girl talking to my big brave friend, and I returned to my condo in awe and at peace.

Love is alive and awake and at one with all that emanates from the great I Am. *We* are alive and awake and at one with all that emanates from the great I Am. Love does not act from fear. So *we* no longer act from fear. Love does not defend itself nor do battle against what gets in the way. Love clears the way by displacing fear. It uses what is there to demonstrate the qualities of love. In the midst of chaos, it remains calm. In the face of betrayal, it remains true. In the arms of uncertainty, it remains certain. Love knows what is real. And love knows what the outcome is.

"And we know that God causes all things to work together for good to those who love God, to those who are called according to His purpose. For those whom He foreknew, He also predestined to become conformed to the image of His Son, so that He would be the firstborn among many brethren," said the Apostle Paul (Romans 8:28–30). God allows us to choose between good and evil. But he knows how we will eventually choose. He did not leave our goodness to chance. He merely stepped back and allowed us opportunity to demonstrate our goodness—not so that he would know that we were good, but so that *we* would know that we were good.

Love is proactive, but in the sense that it goes about *being* love. And when we have reconciled our true self with love, we have nothing to prove. We do not act because we are anxious, feeling a need to do something. We do not act to compete, or to look good, or to make somebody else look bad. We do not act to be accepted, or to make more money, or get more attention. We act only as an extension of love. There really is no "motivation"; we just are the only thing there is to be. Love.

What does that look like in *your* life, though? I think it looks like unconscious competence, like tireless conscious practice of a science coming together with innate artistic talent and the mystery of spirit to make perfection look easy, like what Confucius called *chun tzu*, which can be translated as "humanity-at-its-best." In *The World's Religions,* Huston Smith offers us this explanation of *chun tzu*:

> The *chun tzu* is the opposite of the petty person, a mean person, a small-spirited person. Fully adequate, poised, the *chun tzu* has toward life as a whole the approach of an ideal hostess who is so at home in her surroundings that she is completely relaxed, and, being so, can turn full attention to putting others at their ease. Or to switch genders, having come to the point where he is at home in the universe at large, the *chun tzu* carries these qualities of the ideal host with him through life generally. Armed with a self-respect that generates respect for others, he approaches them

wondering, not, "What can I get from them?" but "What can I do to accommodate them?"

With the hostess's adequacy go a pleasant air and good grace. Poised, confident, and competent, she is a person of perfect address. Her movements are free of brusqueness and violence; her expression is open, her speech free of coarseness and vulgarity. Or to switch genders again, the gentleman does not talk too much. He does not boast, push himself forward, or in any way display his superiority, "except perhaps at sports." Holding always to his own standards, however others may forget theirs, he is never at a loss as to how to behave and can keep a gracious initiative where others resort to conventions. Schooled to meet any contingency "without fret or fear," his head is not turned by success nor his temper soured by adversity.

It is only the person who is entirely real, Confucius thought, who can establish the great foundations of civilized society.

Being "entirely real" means being entirely love! There is nothing great—whether a civilized society or a spiritual movement—that does not begin with the only thing that is real. Love. Everything else is privative; it exists only in the absence of love.

Not surprisingly, Confucius paints a very grown-up picture. And love is all grown-up, but it is at the same time childlike. "Except ye be converted and become as little children, ye shall not enter into the kingdom of heaven," said Jesus (Matthew 18:3). I think Oliver Wendell Holmes would liken it to finding simplicity on the other side of complexity. Abraham Maslow would almost certainly liken it to reaching self-actualization at the top of his hierarchy of needs to find what is truly meaningful in life.

When we reconcile our true self with God to know the oneness of love, we return to our Edenic "paradise." We are not the wise man *or* the innocent child; we are the wise man reborn.

The same Jesus said to seek first the kingdom to find all things. He said that the kingdom is within you. And, yes, he also said that you must be born again to see the kingdom (John 3:3).

There are those who consider Gnostics heretics; others consider Jesus a Gnostic. The Greek word gnosis means knowing through insight or experience (as opposed to scientific knowledge); it involves intuitively understanding oneself. I believe that all great teachers challenge us to choose to know ourselves and, thus, know our God . . . and travail as necessary to give birth to a creature once again born in love, but with the knowledge of good and evil.

As I opened this book, I close it, A scientist, God did not leave our goodness to chance. An artist, he contrasted good with evil, certainty with mystery. And choice is the life he breathed into his creation.

REFERENCES

Academy of Achievement website. *Oprah Winfrey Interview.* Chicago. 21 February 1991.

Mark Aguiar and Erik Hurst. "Measuring Trends in Leisure: The Allocation of Time Over Five Decades." *NBER (National Bureau of Economic Research) Working Paper 12082* (March 2006)

Karen Armstrong. *The Spiral Staircase: My Climb Out of Darkness* (New York: Anchor Books, 2004), Backcover.

Roy F. Baumeister and Mark R. Leary. "The Need to Belong: Desire for interpersonal Attachments as a Fundamental Human Motivation." *Psychological Bulletin* 117 (1995): 497–529.

Frederick Buechner. *Telling Secrets, A Memoir* (New York: HarperCollins Publishers, 1991), 75–76.

CBS Broadcasting Inc. website (2008). New York. 1 December 2006, Story.

CDC (Centers for Disease Control and Prevention) website. 2008.

Dhammapada, as translated by Sangharakshita (New York: Barnes & Noble, 2003), IX, 127.

Sigmund Freud, translated by James Strachey. *Civilization and Its Discontents* (New York: W. W. Norton & Company, 1961), 11.

John M. Gottman Ph.D. and Nan Silver. *Why Marriages Succeed or Fail: And*

How You Can Make Yours Last (New York: Simon & Schuster, 1994), 56–57.

Harville Hendrix. *Getting the Love You Want: A Guide for Couples* (New York: Henry Holt, 1988), 15–19.

Sally Hicks. "Mark Leary on Social Rejection." *Gist from the Mill* (Fall 2007): 15.

James Hossack. "New York's 'Queen of Mean' Leaves $12 Million to Dog." AFP. 29 August 2007.

Amy Iggulden. "Young, Gifted and Trying to Be a Normal Child." *Telegraph. Co.UK,* 2 October 2007, News, 1–3.

Julian Jaynes. *The Origin of Consciousness in the Breakdown of the Bicameral Mind:* (New York: Houghton Mifflin Company, 1976).

Robert Kurzban and Mark R. Leary. "Evolutionary Origins of Stigmatization: The Functions of Social Exclusion." *Psychological Bulletin* 127 no. 2 (2001): 187–208.

Brian Kolodiejchuk, M.C. *Mother Teresa: Come Be My Light* (New York: Doubleday, 2007), 1–2.

Judith H. Langlois and Lori A. Roggman. "Attractive Faces Are Only Average. *Psychological Science* 1 (1990): 115–121.

Mark R. Leary and Deborah L. Downs. "Interpersonal Functions of the Self-esteem Motive: The Self-esteem System as a Sociometer." 123–144 of *Efficacy, Agency, and Self-esteem,* Michael H. Kernis (Berlin: Springer, 1995).

Gary W. Lewandowski, Jr. "Personality Traits Influence Perceived Attractiveness." *Personal Relationships* (December 2007).

Frederick Lane III. *Obscene Profits: The Entrepreneurs of Pornography in the Cyber Age* (New York: Routledge, 2000).

Anne Lamott. *Traveling Mercies: Some Thoughts on Faith* (New York: Random House, 1999).

Edward O. Laumann et al. *The Social Organization of Sexuality: Sexual Practices in the United States* (Chicago: University of Chicago Press, 1994).

Stephen Mitchell. *The Gospel According to Jesus: A New Translation and Guide to His Essential Teachings for Believers and Unbelievers* (New York: Harper-Collins Publishers, 1991), 154.

Thomas Moore. *Original Self* (New York: HarperCollins Publishers, 2000), 25.

NIDDK (National Institute of Diabetes and Digestive and Kidney Diseases) website. 2008.

Cynthia L. Ogden et al. "Mean Body Weight, Height, and Body Mass Index, United States, 1960–2002." *CDC Advance Data From Vital and Health Statistics,* 347, 27 October 2004, 5.

ONDCP (Office of National Drug Control Policy) website (2008). *Fact Sheet.* March 2000.

Elaine Pagels, *Beyond Belief: The Secret Gospel of Thomas,* (New York: Random House, 2003), 143.

Tara Parker-Pope. "Are Kids Getting Too Much Praise?" *New York Times,* 29 October 2007, Health Section, "Well" Column.

James Raffini. *Winners Without Losers: Structures and Strategies for Increasing Student Motivation To Learn.* (Needham Heights, MA: Allyn and Bacon, 1993).

Otto Rank. *A Psychology of Difference: The American Lectures Selected.* Edited, and Introduced by Robert Kramer (Princeton, NJ: Princeton University Press, 1996).

Gill Rhodes et al. "Reflections on Symmetry and Attractiveness." *Psychology, Evolution, and Gender* 1 (1999): 279–295.

John A. Sanford. *The Kingdom Within: The Inner Meaning of Jesus' Sayings,* (New York: HarperCollins Publishers, 1987), 48.

Huston Smith. *Forgotten Truth: The Common Vision of the World's Religions* (New York: HarperCollins Publishers, 1976), 63.

Huston Smith. *The World's Religions: Our Great Wisdom Traditions* (New York: HarperCollins Publishers, 1991), 173.

U.S. Census Bureau website. 2007.

US Census Bureau website. 2008.

Marianne Williamson. *A Return to Love: Reflections on the Principles of A Course in Miracles* (New York: HarperCollins Publishers, 1992), 20.

INDEX

ABOUT THE AUTHOR

JAN DENISE is a nationally syndicated newspaper columnist and the author of *Naked Relationships: Sharing Your Authentic Self to Find the Partner of Your Dreams.* Grateful for the chance to inspire others to know the best of who they are—the best of life and love—she conducts workshops, speaks professionally, and consults with individuals and couples. She lives on a farm and intimate retreat center in McIntosh, Florida, where she is silly and deeply in love with life and her husband. To learn more, visit her website at www.NakedRelationships.com.

EXPERIENCE THE LAW OF ATTRACTION

Jack Canfield provides intelligent anecdotes, exercises and action steps, giving you everything you need to create the life you desire.

Jack Canfield's KEY
to Living the
Law of Attraction

A Simple Guide to
Creating the Life of Your Dreams

Jack Canfield *and* D.D. Watkins

Code #6586 • $19.95

Gratitude
A Daily Journal

Honor and Appreciate
the Abundance in Your Life

Jack Canfield *and* D.D. Watkins

Code #7108 • $19.95

This must-have companion journal provides a month-by-month layout and serves as a valuable tool in bringing about positive change in your life.